A
GROWING
GARDENER

A GROWING GARDENER

ABBIE ZABAR

UNIVERSE

First published in the United States of America in 1996
by UNIVERSE PUBLISHING
A Division of Rizzoli International Publications, Inc.
300 Park Avenue South
New York, NY 10010

Text, drawings, calligraphy, compilation copyright © 1996 Abbie Zabar

Portions of "Allen Haskell, Horticulturist" appeared in slightly different form in *Hortus*.

96 97 98 99 / 10 9 8 7 6 5 4 3 2 1

Printed by Tien Wah Press in Singapore

Library of Congress Cataloging-in-Publication Data

Zabar, Abbie.
    A growing gardener / written, illustrated, and designed by Abbie
Zabar.
        p.   cm.
    ISBN 0-7893-0035-4
    1. Gardening—New York (State)—New York. 2. Gardens—New York
(State)—New York.   3. Zabar, Abbie.   I. Title.
SB455.Z33 1996
635.9'86'097471—dc20   96-19432
                                                                  CIP

Cover: The pot on the front cover is from Impruneta, a town in the hills just south of Florence, where twelfth-generation artisans continue to produce vessels the color of a Tuscan sunrise. The hand-finished decorative terra cotta pot is filled with grape hyacinths, *Muscari armeniacum,* because, as the Persian saying goes, "If you have two loaves of bread, sell one and buy a hyacinth" to feed your soul. On the spine is *Anomatheca laxa,* a South African bulb that produces a bright coral red flower. The back cover is a small Sussex trug of hickory wood, with an end-of-day crop of cherry tomatoes.

Title page: Flowering chives, *Allium senescens*
Inscription page: A pot of oats for the cat
Table of contents: Four seasons of *Taxus × media* 'Brownii'

Allow yourself to become what has so graciously been given to you. (A Trappist Monk)

WINTER

SPRING

SUMMER

AUTUMN

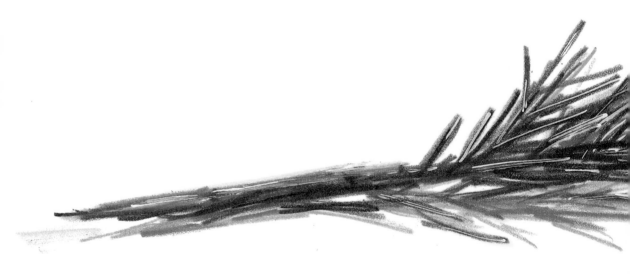

It is said, "Rosemary only grows where the mistress is master."

PROLOGUE

GARDENING SOLITUDE SUITS ME. ⅍ I'M SITTING on the ground, spellbound by something I don't remember planting. It's a little flash of green making tracks along the crack in one of my stone urns, where the guy who moved it also broke it. Or I catch crocus leaves plowing through the last snow of the season and I'm gaping at sights as if they were the outtakes in a porno movie. I don't mean to get personal, but do you know anything more pleasurable than watching eternal optimism front row, center? ⅍ My contained garden dares to grow in a chaotic city, probably because I have the pluck to cultivate a rooftop beneath the heavens, over the fumes of traffic, and in between schedules and scaffolds of construction crews. I'm working twenty-one stories above asphalt and cement while reaching for the moon and the stars; Eden is not without effort. ⅍ Neatly sheared evergreen walls—no higher than the building's parapet— emphasize my garden's constraints. As well as its strengths. I've got forty-four running feet of tightly sheared *Taxus* x *media* 'Brownii' hedge for backbone because I prefer slow-growing hardwood in plants as well as people. Or maybe I just want a green ledge for drying laundry in the summertime because I also love it when the sheets smell of sunshine. ⅍ If I remember, that was twenty-two muddy, burlapped root-balls, each humped up the extra flight of stairs since not one of these elevators goes to the roof. ⅍ I know back-hall mea-

"Meeting adversity well is the source of your strength."
(Lucky numbers 1, 3, 5, 20, 27, 42)
(Fortune Cookie, 1995)

surements like my own. Door widths and stairwell turns are as cozy to me as my bathtub. Stop moaning—it beats trying to get something going down on the street. There trees are fair game for dogs, annuals don't last an hour, and new plantings are mulched by broken glass from the last parade, plus it's all harnessed with locks and chains of hardened steel. Or in the country, where starving deer—simply doing what comes naturally in order to survive winter—eat everything from spiny rose canes to soft saplings down to the ground. Not my problems. I share this garden with hard-hat crews. For years every contractor in the yellow pages has been hammer-drilling through membranes meant to be waterproof, ripping apart parapet walls about to fall down, or giving silicone fixes to where the caulking between the cross-mortar joints is still missing. Riggers are moving my planters and they've got cords and cables and electrical extension wires limbing my trees and strangling the shrubbery. But why should I expect them to respect life when demolition is their business? Dealing with concrete, cement, and stone every day puts them in a very hard place. 🌿
I ask you, is this any way to garden? For over twenty years, it's the only way I know how. No wonder I'm rooting for what's coming through the crevice. Plantings occur randomly out there, cropping up

The timber of the taxus is tough and strong, but new growth is soft and feathery.

wherever they can. But nature doesn't make gardens—
we do. So I'm going to cultivate that little emerald emis-
sary, prune off any straggly growth, and, every now and then,
add a pinch of plant food. ❧ Some people I know look down
their noses at gardens not grown in the ground. Or won't forgive
your topsoil if it comes in plastic bags, not from double digging. But
if Paradise—from the ancient Persian *pairidaeza*—was originally nothing more than a walled enclosure for protection from sand and wind in
the desert, why were they futzing around with lilies, violets, lilacs,
evening-blooming primroses, jasmine, and roses—especially roses—
brought back from plant expeditions from all around the world? Or
the reflecting pools with tinkling jets of water surrounded by shim-
mering allées of broad-leafed trees—mere irrigation? In hostile envi-
ronments, who wouldn't crave the fragrant aromas, be nourished by
the song of nightingales, or suckle up to sounds of dribbling water?
❧ Fifteen thousand years ago Manhattan was a towering wall of ice
and today I grow tender green above some eight hundred acres of
lawns, lakes, ponds, and trees. I'm looking at wide-open space and
the best man-made panorama is in my face. Yet my garden is a humble plan, ennobled by the grandeur of New York City's Central Park.
I bow to one of civilization's most dramatic backdrops. Alberti, the
fifteenth-century Florentine architect and scholar—epitome of the
Renaissance man—believed that villa, garden, and site should form a
harmonious whole and recommended using "surrounding hills as your
own." The ancient Romans did that all the time and called it
working with "familiar mountains." The way I look at it,
I'm just borrowing some bushes from the yard across the

"What is paradise? But a garden,
an orchard of trees and herbs,
full of pleasure and nothing
there but delights."
(William Lawson, "The Country
Housewife's Garden," 1617,
the first gardening book written
expressly for women)

has succulent

Foraging for edible weeds: pungent purslane

street that's more than two miles long. How Trouble is the neighbor I've got behind me—his place is an eyesore. It's where the landlord piles the debris, and some weeks, before they cart it away, it looks and smells like a landfill operation. But when pipe-and-board scaffolding, demolition gear, or mechanics, riggers, hard-hat crews, and even firemen—plus city inspectors logging the violations—aren't all over the roof, that's when crevices start collecting things and then I call it "the meadow." How spectacular to see the way nature moves in. Left fallow and untrampled for months, weeds return, followed by insects, and eventually the birds. I could be watching alluvial soil in Australia, where I'm told it's gold-bearing. In no time a standard-order pebble-over-tar top becomes a mat of shallow-rooted violas, wild strawberries, sedum, and purslane for my salads, which just today I noticed they were getting $2.50 a quarter of a pound for at the Farmer's Market. Christ Almighty! I feel like a Buddhist when it comes to preserving every scrappy bit of vegetation. But for just a bunch of weeds in a setting that might all be pulled up tomorrow, I'd say they're doing a swell job in a no-win situation. Think I'll serve *them* a little plant food too. Making way for green is nothing new. Even in New York. Frederick Law Olmsted, designer of Central Park was also planner of record for the promenades of Riverside Park, built over freight-train tracks. Battery Park City sits on acres of landfill. Before the World Fairs, Corona Park was a garbage dump. Most recently, in exchange for allowing a sewage treatment plant to be built in Harlem, residents got Riverbank State Park. So now on a hot summer day 15,000 people—without their own backyards—have

"The thing generally raised on city land is taxes." (Charles Dudley Warner, "My Summer in a Garden," 1870)

...aves that can be sautéed with minced garlic and rosemary to spread on grilled French bread.

brick-paved esplanades, old-fashioned benches, and evergreens and honey locust trees on top of a sewage treatment plant. Hooray for eternal optimism. We live in times when the mercury is rising. Tell them New York is dealing with global warming. When they're playing hockey in the streets with Combat cockroach disks or the Brooklyn Botanic Garden encourages inner-city kids to turn some soil, but the instructions with the freebie morning glory seeds say "try planting in a window box and letting the vine grow up the bars," ain't it the truth? Yet gardens will always be made in spite of the odds, because sometimes I suspect Eden is more

From Dominick's office, 43rd floor of the Empire Sta

a process than a place. 🌿 In California they're having droughts and in Wisconsin it's flooding. Hurricanes hit Florida. Tornadoes take Kansas and the Mississippi River is misbehaving all over the Midwest. Or another earthquake does L.A. before lunch. Moi? I'm sitting tight, praying the glass in my rattling windows won't explode the way it did the last time. I try like hell to ignore the breeze, but up here it's not whispering pines. After howling for days, it sounds like the world's coming to an end. I go to bed and maybe if the 60-mile-an-hour winds die down I'll get some sleep. 🌿 The next morning I could be dreaming. The air's so still that I catch early summer birdsong, and once again a gardener learns to make peace with what she's got. I'm watching my resident red-tailed hawk take the wife and kiddies out for a spin on some thermal air currents. I was happy to read that those birds mate for life. Maybe not gardens, but at least some things are forever. Ecstatic little sparrows are cropping my woolly thyme for nest batting and monarch butterflies will be back to sunbathe on the Russian sage; the bees will go for any flower that's purple and in September I'll smell the sweet autumn clematis. Yes, I hear trickling water in a hot Persian garden. In fact, I reckon I'm working Paradise. 🌿 Gardens are the world of today and a wish for tomorrow. A chance to capture the redeeming qualities in down-to-earth miracles. You bet the soil is pay dirt. 🌿

"Life is always a rich and steady time when you are waiting for Something to happen or hatch."
(Charlotte to Wilbur, E.B. White, "Charlotte's Web," 1952)

...uilding, looking South toward Madison Square Park

" It is forbidden to live in a Town which has no greenery"

no lot in the great fraternity of those who watch the changing
how can they keep warm their hearts in winter?"

(Mrs. Francis King, "Pages from a Garden Notebook," 1921)

WINTER

I FEED MY CAT, I BOIL SOME WATER, AND things are looking good because the sky over where the sun is rising reminds me of morning glories, 'Heavenly Blue' variety. ✻ I put on a down vest over the men's flannel shirt I sometimes sleep in, the wool cap I hardly ever wear because it's too warm but I don't tell my mother since it's what she knitted me for Christmas, then a pair of knee-high socks and my mud boots because they don't need lacing when I'm rushing—but nothing else. Now I hope the doorbell doesn't ring, since no one's going to believe that I'm busy working and sometimes this is what I wear to work. I grab a pair of clippers, my favorite shears, and the long-handled pruners—the kind they use in orchards—which are what I like for loppers when you need the extra reach or when branches are too thick. I'm also carrying the small eighteenth-century silver skittle-ball teapot—bachelor-size, it's called—plus a plate with the two chocolate croissants Mme Bonté slipped in while we were talking and I wasn't looking when I picked up the petits fours last night. ✻ Energy is coming from the ground and the breath of balmy weather can pass for a spunky imitation of spring. The pulse bobs through my blood and budded limbs are as promising as wishbones. The darkest time of the year has come and gone, days of light are up and about, and I'm springier than a grasshopper in the crackling brightness. The mood in the air is contagious, but not the stuff you're liable to catch on the downside of the solstice. 🌿 Two little creatures chatting up a storm on a branch in the new row of European hornbeams, *Carpinus betulus* 'Fastigiata', tell me something's going on. It blows my mind how those young whips—so skinny they don't even throw a shadow—support birds that are all chest and belly. At the same time I'm thinking, Where the hell were those critters last fall? 🌿 I'd say I'm a neat person. I like a tidy garden, I sweep after I prune. Coffee containers, sugar wrappers, cigarette butts—that's my mess after construction crews dismantle the scaffolds and call it a day. But in September when sparrows are picking at the red hips, spitting out what they don't want, and pooping all over the place, I wouldn't clean up after them for anything. Signs of life like that make me smile. Or, as the early-twentieth-century American poet and gardener Celia

"But clutter and mess
show us life is being lived."
(Anne Lamott,
"Bird by Bird," 1994)

"The Art of Fine Baking," 1961)
(Paula Peck,
"Each little cake needs no more than the tiniest bit of decoration."

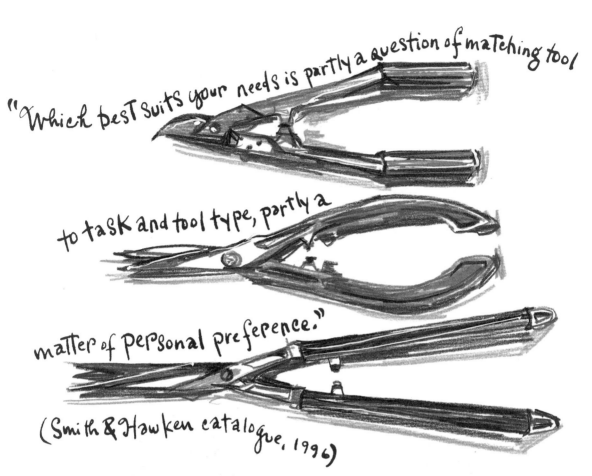

"Which best suits your needs is partly a question of matching tool to task and tool type, partly a matter of personal preference."

(Smith & Hawken catalogue, 1996)

Thaxter said, "How should they know the garden was not planted for them?" The air is tempting, there is no wind—no wind?—and I'm inhaling a moment from a long-lost season. Any gardener not big on stalling knows today's when I show the Washington hawthorns, *Crataegus phaenopyrum,* who's boss. But before I had a little talk with myself, I honestly thought about putting it off until tomorrow. It's how I drag my feet with everything important. Especially if I'm holding my favorite pen, there's ink in the cartridge, and the bird I want to draw is in front of me standing still. Suddenly I need to check out the one-day sale in the shoe department at Bergdorf's, even if I only wear clogs. ❦ They say pruning during dormancy gives vigorous new growth in spring. It's before the energy and sap are flowing, and all my trees still have some winter sleep in their eyes. I also figure if I prune today I'll have the best shot at eliminating the parasitic water sprouts that suck out more energy than they give back. Usually they pop up after pruning a major limb, because when you cut into healthy wood you're initiating growth from dormant buds, and in general the most vigorous developments come from the severest surgery. ❦ But water sprouts are like relatives from the side of the family no one talks to. Not only do they look like losers, they have no social manners. They move in and take over the crown of the tree, filling up the nice clean space you've been saving for someone you'd really like to invite. A couple of birds building a nest, maybe. ❦ I want my hawthorns to have solar-friendly crowns, open in the middle, not so crowded that every branch is competing for elbowroom and light. And I'd like them to form canopies above my head the way trees did when I was two feet tall. I want limbs to layer so that the leaves will shingle, like on a roof. Not rub up as strangers do on the subway at rush hour. Crisscrossing branches with thorns everywhere you look—and you thought the name was just a coincidence—cause chafing. Chafing wounds the bark, and open bark is like a vacancy sign to passing insects, and I'm already entertaining bugs big-time in the season, thank you. ❦ So I'm up there with my head and shoulders in the twiggiest hawthorn tree, and god bless my mother's hat, knitted with double skeins of wool, so thick my brain is padded. I'm getting good height standing on the top step of the ladder, where it says

"Birds are as important as plants in my garden."
(Anne Scott-James, "Gardening Letters to My Daughter," 1990)

"Do not stand at or above this level," even though the sentence "**YOU CAN LOSE YOUR BALANCE**" is in boldfaced caps. With no leaves and without shadows I see bunches of dried-up cedar-rust cankers left over from the summertime. Something else to infect the bark and the surrounding tissue and make me wonder why I like gardening so much. The cankerous growths come by way of my spiral junipers, *Juniperus* x *media* 'Hetz's Columnaris', but since I'm not ready to give up the host plants, I'll just cut off the diseased branches. ⚘ Pruning is a necessary process that removes the unnecessary. Nature does it automatically but arbitrarily, like when storms and heavy snow loads break limbs off trees and shrubs. Or you know how the city plants its sycamores right near a bus stop and every day another branch snaps? That's one way of limbing. But the good news is we can prune on purpose. Besides removing dead, damaged, or diseased parts, new budding will be stimulated by concentrating the editing effort where it is most wanted. ⚘ One morning, before I was into all this pruning stuff, there was a leftover pot of rosemary on the sidewalk, because who wants a plant that's supposed to be bushy at the bottom but isn't? I was thinking, If it's still there when I get back from the post office—and you know how long that can be—then that orphan was meant for me. ⚘ Next I'm standing over the sink and turning the little rosemary round and around; I'm doing my own limbing up, removing more and more branches from the bottom until I've got a tiny tree. One with a very little trunk. Branches don't move upward when a tree grows taller, the way your arms did when you were a kid and you were growing. A tree grows from the top, so the lowest branch on a five-foot tree will always be at five feet. Unless you

* One of the main challenges of coaching is to get players to do what they don't want in order to achieve what they do want."
(Pat Riley, former New York Knicks coach, 1992)

prune it off. But you can only prune so much before you're left with nothing. Like most of life, it's a delicate balance: you want to define the form yet leave enough material to nourish what's there, and then just do a bit of shaping now and then.
🌿 That's why pruning should be done early in the development of the plant, limb, or shoot. Try to give something direction before it's too late. The best shot at getting the desired effects, as well as saving and steering growth, is to start pruning while still in the nursery. It might only mean rubbing out bud eyes, but the goal is to form good stock early on. 🌿 That rosemary nobody wanted became my first topiary standard, after the fact. It will never be tall and elegant, but that's not to say it isn't winsome. Far as I'm concerned, I made a big deal out of nothing, and doesn't that count for something? 🌿

"As for rosemarie, I lette it runne all over my garden walls, not onlie because my bees love it, but because it is the herb sacred to remembrance and to frendship." (Thomas More, English statesman, 16thc.)

Taking Note

"Why do all my best ideas come to me shaving?" (Albert Einstein, 20th c. physicist)

I AGREE WITH BENJAMIN FRANKLIN: "MAKE RECOLLECTION AS durable as possible—put it down on paper." I also think, "Just get it down. You'll get a grip later." ✹ That's why I wind up with insights on the outsides of grocery bags or I'm drawing the garden at the Frick Collection on the back of a fax I just picked up. Maybe it would be more impressive if I told you I write my notes in journals with marble endpapers handmade in a little shop in Venice, but I seem to work better on paper not bound like a book before there's much to say. Any scrap that's handy is more my style of the moment. ✹ Luckily I jotted down the date in late fall when I pruned the watersprouts off my hawthorn trees because, as it turns out, it wasn't late enough. You'd imagine by November everything would be tired of growing, but those suckers? They came right back. So now I'm going to try again, before the sap is rising, when there's a January thaw and it's warm enough to grab my loppers, go outside, and do what I have to do. If that works, sure I want it in writing—gold leaf maybe. ✹ Plant tags are okay, but mine always get misplaced, then crop up later in the wrong pot. Besides, if you ever had markers big enough to record all the lengthy sagas and histories of each plant, you'd be looking at a landscape of labels. ✹ Whether you garden in the mud or the mind, plan it on paper or plant it right away, notes are a down-to-earth tool. With the bragging and complaining there is careful observation, and if I'm gardening by the book, my own perceptions are good for starts. ✹ There was the February when I scribbled

"Don't forget to pick up a packet of 'Heavenly Blues'" because the year before they ran out of morning glory vines before I got to the nursery. In April, I noted, I nicked twenty seeds with my box cutter, which now they're saying is the weapon of choice in city schools for the same reason I use it: it's small, it's sharp, and it has a retractable blade. Probably next year when box cutters are off the market, I'll be thankful I added "sandpaper is good for scratching hard-coated seeds if you want to make them absorb water easily" when I heard that tip. I also recorded that after soaking the seeds overnight they were soft and looking more like something with a future. I thought it was silly to write down that it made me feel the way I did back in the fifth grade, when the mold was coming along nicely on the stale bread in my science project, but that's the way I felt. I planted my morning glory seeds in the commercial cardboard eggflats I always see stacked in the kitchen of the diner around the corner, because they look more like propagating trays to me. I put the set-up on a windowsill upstairs to germinate, and a few weeks later I had a nursery. On May 10 I wrote that I'd transplanted each seedling outside to the stone planters beneath the railings. Another memo reminded me it was the same day I sowed the remaining packet of seeds in situ. No nicking, no presoaking, no nothing. Just wanted to see if following instructions made a difference. That summer there

"What I want is less of my thoughts and more of my feelings." (Joel Meyerowitz, photographer, "Cape Light," 1978)

were so many morning glories, who had time for notes? ⚘ Last March, when I planted seeds of "living stones," *Lithops* (from the Greek words *lithos,* meaning stone, and *ops,* meaning face) I was taking notes like crazy because all the books tell you how hard it is to propagate lithops from seed without a greenhouse; plus, when the package says "Some Experience Useful" you know it's not going to be Radishes 101. I sprinkled my lithops seeds—the size of pepper grinds—over sand in a small aluminum tray with a clear plastic cover, the kind you get when dinner's coming from the salad bar at the Korean grocery. Every morning I'd check to see if something had grown overnight, because nothing can make or break a gardener's day quicker than doing a head count as soon as the sun is rising. But right from the beginning these guys are hiding. Living stones are mimicry plants with succulent little bodies that hold water and take the place of leaves and not a bad idea to be pebble look-alikes if you grow between sand and gravel in the desert and don't want to be eaten. ⚘ By the end of summer I had twelve seedlings—that's from two packages with twenty-eight seeds each—and today I only have six. ⚘ They look just like a bunch of stones, nestled among itty-bitty gravel in my tiniest trough—a cut-stone match-strike-and-holder I bought because it looked like a rock but wasn't. (Isn't anything around here what it's supposed to be?) But this spring, I've got my notes, I've got the "useful experience" part, and I go with Martin Luther's testament of faith: "Even if I knew the world would end tomorrow I'd continue to plant my apple trees." ⚘

"Multum in Parvo" (Latin for "much in little.")

"On picking up from the stony ground what was supposed a curiously shaped pebble, it proved to be a plant... but in color and appearance bore the closest resemblance to the stones between which it was growing."

"A minute's success pays the failure of years." (Robert Browning, "Apollo and the Fates," 1886)

Something
keeping a
my sanse-
I started from
sent me in the
uncle's green-
she didn't have
house the moment
without it. Here's
like because its
is written all over
tolerate abuse and
and that's why they're
worth's or why I re-
the basement window
a gorgeous twenty-year-

else I was
record of was
vieria, which
divisions Tovah
mail from her
house, because
any in her green-
I couldn't live
another plant I
struggle to survive
its face. Sansevierias
thrive on neglect,
selling them at Wool-
member seeing one in
of a Chinese laundry,
old specimen that no one

ever watered (that was doing great because no one ever watered). Don't you love it when hoity-toity people—who know zilch about plants—are snobs when something's not the Johnny-come-lately of the orchid world? What a wonder when a little hoi polloi number, given the right situation, grows finer than what seems rare. 🌿 I was growing the spear kind, *Sansevieria cylindrica,* which ends in a point, like an agave in the desert. The tip is sharp enough to impale a visitor coming through the window who maybe wasn't invited; what was once abundant foliage has evolved into the architecture of leaves shaped like strong green husks. 🌿 After several years and three pottings-up later, someone who "knows" said my plant looked like a

"I have always thought a kitchen garden a more pleasant sight than the finest orangery or artificial greenhouse." (Joseph Addison, "The Spectator," September 6, 1712)

(William J. Burchell, "Travels in the Interior of Southern Africa," 1822-1824)

"Once I drew like Raphael, but it has taken a whole life time to learn to draw like children."
(Pablo Picasso, 20th c. artist)

winner, and could probably take a blue ribbon in the plant curios category at the New York Flower Show. That was even before it flowered. Thank St. Fiacre, patron saint of gardeners, that in between rinsing the arugula and feeding my cat I took a moment to sketch the sansevieria when it was in bloom. The bottle-brush inflorescence was filling the house at night with a delicate fragrance, letting me know it's probably pollinated by a nocturnal insect—maybe my friend the moth. But last summer—August 6, to be exact—right after the silicone crew working on the other side of the building did a broadcast spraying with chemicals that were meant for sealing masonry in the hope of closing pores and making the brickwork waterproof, one of the first plants to turn black and start shriveling up was my spear sansevieria—the one I was growing because it's supposed to be a fighter. I was trying not to cry when I showed the other dead and defenseless parts of my garden to the contractor and building management, but they all looked at me like I was crazy, like "Woman! go talk to a tree." Why, the foreman swore his workers weren't even near my terrace. Exactly! 🌿 Wanna hear a strange coincidence? My plants became silicone casualties on the fiftieth anniversary of dropping the largest bomb ever used in warfare. The A-bomb was only meant for civilians in Hiroshima, but sixteen miles away human beings had peeling flesh hanging from their bodies, missing ears, and deformed fingers, and who knows what else went wrong after that mushroom in the sky. 🌿 As well as the accomplishments and achievements, gardening is filled with disasters and disappointments. That's why I go back to my notes to remember the past or conjure up future gardens where everything still seems possible.

I'm moving some containers and replanting others, even though I haven't gotten up from my seat in front of the window in over an hour. I'm so itchy to start all over again I could be one of those pitch pine cones after the wildfire on Long Island that needed extraordinary heat to crack their seals, expose their seeds, and get things going. The blaze consumed 5,500 acres of tinder-dry woods and took 2,200 firefighters to put it out; it also uncovered seedlings which never before saw sunlight, seedlings that probably wouldn't have had a shot at germinating if they'd remained in the shade of those tall trees. At the bottom of her Christmas letter, Helen, who lives fifteen minutes from the center of the Pine Barrens conflagration, added a little note which I pasted next to my own notes to remind me that there will always be a spark of life in the ruins— if you're paying attention. "It's amazing that between the awful black stumps green sprouts have already started," she wrote.

"My pictures are often made by a sum of destructions."
(Pablo Picasso)

"A garden never looks perfect; Something is always dying, Something else about to bloom."
(Nigel Nicolson, Son of Vita Sackville-West and Harold Nicolson, 1993)

The fragrance of forced freesias, blooming on New Years Day!

Books

JEN, IMPRESSED BY MY "GARDEN LIBRARY," ASKED ME TO TELL her about it. "Library"? Those books chose me. ✒ The child who read by flashlight in the middle of the night? Under the covers? Not Abbie. I don't know about your education, but far as the classics went I never even read the Cliffs Notes. Besides, the whole idea of "collecting" has me ready to dust. ✒ But you know when something racy grabs you—say the multicultural appeal of cross-stitch embroidery or Pomo Indian baskets or the winter migration of monarch butterflies—the next thing, stuff you never knew was out there is everywhere. I've been getting catalogues on gardening books from England, France, and Germany—and "gesundheit" is still all I know in German—because one day I needed more than botanical nomenclature. Now I have dirt under the fingernails but I'm on a first-name basis with rare-book dealers I used to call "Monsieur." ✒ That isn't to say the first time I visited Elisabeth Woodburn, the doyenne of antiquarian books on horticulture, it was easy. I was taken to her Booknoll Farm by a guy who gardened for a living but also dug flowery books, and everyone knew so much more than I did that I sat on a little footstool the whole afternoon, eyeing spines of *incunabula* before I could even pronounce the word. But the doyenne became my encouraging friend and resource for what I never knew I needed. From her shelves came *Histoire des tulipes,* a palm-size treasure with hand-colored stipple engravings by Pancrace Bessa, one of the great early-nineteenth-century botanical artists. Or how about the humble brown

"'Classic.' A book which people praise and don't read."
(Mark Twain, "Following the Equator," 1897)

"But no matter how good a book is, it isn't worth anything until you're ready for it."
(Anne Raver, garden writer, 1995)

"Plain shelves filled with good editions in good bindings are more truly decorativ

paper-over-board number that's been my design muse for so much of what I do it's about time I give credit: *The Little Pruning Book, An Intimate Guide to the Surer Growing of Better Fruits and Flowers,* which was "published in the interest of better gardening by the Peck, Stow and Wilcox Co., Makers of Quality Pruning Shears, Cleveland, Ohio, 1917." It's probably something the nurseries gave away, like nowadays when you get a beer mug at the local gas station just for filling up. 🌿 One bibliography page leads to another, so luckily I'm not growing one of everything because I don't want an arboretum of books. Gertrude Jekyll said you could have a collection of plants and still not have a garden. 🌿 I see horticulture through the eyes of an artist, not the lens of a botanist. Drawings of sectional plant studies—framed in debossed platemarks—give me inspiration, not information. I like toothy, deckle-edged papers of 100 percent rag with watermarks you can see when the light comes through, or gilt-edged pages to keep the insides from getting buggy and dusty. I enjoy the bumps left by deep impressions of hand-set type that make each word seem weighty. And if it isn't asking too much, please don't remove the miniature seal—the little "ticket"—that old-time bookstores always used to paste on the bottom of the inside cover. I

"One for facts, one for ideas, one for amusement, one for ecstasy. I have been pondering on which four books I would choose for a learner—that the beginner, though ignorant of gardening, would be otherwise literate." (Anne Scott-James, "Gardening Letters to My Daughter," 1990)

"I'd leave all the hurry, the noise, and the fray, for a house full of books and a garden of flowers." (Andrew Lang, Scottish scholar and man of letters)

...an ornate bookcases with tawdry books." (Edith Wharton, "The Decoration of Houses," 1902)

FROM THE GARDEN LIBRARY OF ABBIE ZABAR

want it more than any self-important ex libris from some previous owner. I'm happy with my own bit of a bookplate—one inch by one inch, and engraved. 🌿 As far as bindings go, unless it came from the shelves of the Bodleian Library or the Vatican or the Morgan, I prefer things in their original duds. I don't want what new money is doing to old books. Only when a fragile work must be preserved do I have a slipcase made, and then I like plain linen-and-flax paper over museum board, and a thin pull of unassuming binder's tape so the book won't ever have to be shaken out again. It's been through enough already. 🌿 We live in times when the corner reading room is at the mall sharing gonzo real estate with the cineplex, and volumes of rare botanical-plate books are broken apart because they've become more valuable as wallpaper than between their cover boards. I don't do stuff like that, but I'll scribble shoulder memos and marginalia without remorse. I'm having little discussions with the author, and when friends say my sidebars make for an even better read, I mark it up to a different take on book appreciation. Personal provenance adds soul, and I'm grateful for signs of life. 🌿 I want to remember if my book came by way of yard sale, auction, or friend. *Wild and Old Garden Roses* was a thank-you from a woman whose private garden library in Virginia is probably the best in America. And all I have to do is open a first edition of Eleanour Sinclair Rohde's *Rose Recipes* (1939), with the faded bouquet of black violas pressed inside, and just like that we're lying under the camellias on a hillside and he's proposing, even while the man I was married to is waiting for me down in the valley. 🌿 In the spring of 1976 I saw an ad for an

"Reading the text together with the commentary is like eavesdropping and carries the same guilty pleasure." (Allen Lacy, "Farther Afield," 1986)

"In strong winds the trunk would sway in a sinuous motion which combined the suppleness of a snake with the strength of an elephant."
(Anne LaBastille, "Woodswomen," 1976)

rod meant for reinforcing concrete—down alongside the trunk of a containerized tree, straight through until it hits bottom. Then three or four guy wires are looped fairly high into the crown and pegged at ground level a few feet from the central stem to prevent the tree from blowing over before the roots have taken hold in the earth. The trunk is wrapped so it won't get chafed against the stake, and all support material is loosely tied to avoid scarring the bark. Eventually after a few seasons it's essential to cut the wires and chuck the props.

🌿 Like the rest of us, a tree must stabilize itself while learning to bend in the wind. 🌿

...ather than conventional stakes, cables, and guy wires, allows natural movement of a young sapling.

The winter is past, the pain is over and gone; the flowers appear on the earth; the time of

singing of birds is come, and the voice of the turtle is heard in our land. (The Song of Solomon 2: 10-12)

SPRING

I'M HEARING LITTLE HOUSE SPARROWS, *Passer domesticus.* ✒ A bunch of them are nosing around under the hornbeams, the windbreak I've got growing on the twenty-first floor of an apartment building, because up here the wind is serious and so am I when it comes to protecting my garden. Their chirps sound like squeaky shears and remind me I better re-oil the loppers and pruners, which also makes me think it's not too long now. Tell me please, what is the first—I mean really the first—sign of spring in these parts? ✒ Was it a few days after the winter solstice when I was walking crosstown early in the morning, and streaks of rising sun turned skyscrapers into a twentieth-century Stonehenge? Or was it some weeks later, back around the end of January, when one of Central Park's resident red-tailed hawks, *Buteo jamaicensis,* flew by my terrace, talons tight around a branch? ✒ But maybe spring is when the Callery pears—not the species *Pyrus communis* that produce edible fruit, but *Pyrus calleryana,* the ornamental kind—are about to flower on every street. Limbs are loaded with buds. Big-deal heavy oversized heads are out of proportion to the caliper of graceless trunks, and fast-growing, brittle wood creates weak crotches and something will snap even before the garbage truck backs up. Make it through another urban winter, and Callery pears become nothing short of the city's horticultural harbinger of spring. The early froth of white flow-

"Spring has arrived. It is no use your telling me to look at the calendar. This morning, beyond a shadow of a doubt, I saw the spring." (Amy Lowell, early 20th c. poet)

ers crowns them the unofficial winner in the street-tree category, so
we forgive them everything. In a couple of weeks their calcimine
light will haze out urban blight the way the first day of a blizzard
does it for us in winter. ✌ Those birds, the ones with the chirps I
told you about, are pulling at my woolly thyme. *Thymus hirsutus minus*
is a ground cover that's downy, soft, and aromatic—and what the parents want near their chicks. It looks the way it feels, the way some
words sound like what they mean. ✌ Around here birds are making
house calls and constructing nests in the open ends of steel pipes
hanging over traffic, in the top loop of the *B* in the Citibank sign
around the corner, and in all the crannies between the air conditioners
and the sills that the rest of us never gave a thought to. ✌ Sure, I
know how farmers consider the little brown birds to be agricultural
pests because they eat the grain growing in the fields and stored in
the sheds. Besides, everyone else is angry at the sparrows—and the
starlings too—for taking over the eastern bluebird's nesting boxes.
✌ But maybe my ornithology inferiority complex is showing again.
I'm thinking that all the people out there with the binoculars and the
gardeners who don't depend on soil in plastic bags are getting flocks
of better birds. Me? I'm just grateful to little brown sparrows I can
watch every month of the year without the fancy accessories, because

"Connaissance et Culture Parfaite des Belles Fleurs" (1696) recommended

any kind of bird is an inexpensive and efficient barometer. You bet I'll share my woolly thyme. 🌿 It poured so heavily last night that I've got earthworms covering my terrace because they all crawled out of the soil when they needed more oxygen. Now they need a lift to get back home. I pick up the ones that are still alive and squiggling, not easy for a native city daughter. I set them on the woolly thyme, but in case they still don't get the message I'm starting the holes for them, because maybe they've been away so long they've forgotten how to tunnel. It's when I see that the ground cover is thicker than my doormat, and the stems are so hairy that the rain just beaded up on the leaves. Makes me wonder how the hornbeam roots are ever going to get any water. Is it spring when I've forgotten about blizzards and I'm worrying whether there'll be a drought this summer? 🌿 I'm going down to buy some supplies from the back of the truck with the evergreens and the annuals staged on tiers the way seventeenth-century Flemish flower growers displayed pots of early-blooming auriculas. Starting now that truck will be parked around the corner every day, bringing Eden—as well as bags of topsoil—to the hinterlands. So if I don't see anything else I need, I'll be back, because spring is really about tomorrow. 🌿

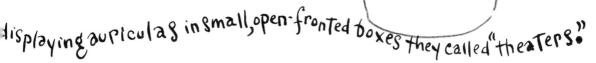

displaying auriculas in small, open-fronted boxes they called "theaters."

Allen Haskell, Horticulturist

IMAGINE A RETAIL PLANT NURSERY WHERE, BEYOND THE visitor's parking area, white peacocks languidly groom their alabaster feathers, lovebirds share a private dovecote under a cascade of umbels flowing from a forty-foot climbing vine of *Hydrangea anomala petiolaris,* and upright Japanese yews, *Taxus cuspidata* 'Robusta', rise like our Northeast answer to the Mediterranean cypress. ✿ Allen Haskell's "rare and unusual plants and plantings of distinction," as his stationary reads, is quixotically sited behind the drystone wall with granite pillars, just down the road from the Shawmut Diner when you get off Interstate 95 in New Bedford, Massachusetts. But the first time I went there I was still married, which meant we flew over in my husband's plane. ✿ That was eighteen years ago, and now it's the beginning of June, the time of year when containerized perennials are neatly set within rectangular beds—like parterre gardening—and potted annuals are color-coordinated so that your design eye kicks in even if you never studied art, or landscaping for that matter. ✿ I got here late today, just in

time to wash my hands and throw water on my face. We sit down with margaritas in the cool evening breeze on the open stone terrace, part of the landmarked 1725 Federal farmhouse at the northerly end of Allen Haskell's property, one of seven original farmsteads that created this vernacular

New England setting. The damp blanket of air rolling in from the Atlantic Ocean is tomorrow morning's dew, and the resident cats have finished dinner and now they're licking their paws as if they were popsicles. A frosty pitcher of sangria is passed around before we tackle Gene's homemade lobster salad with huge chunks of white meat on toasted pita bread from the neighborhood bakery, and Allen is serving up some of his own food-thinking. He'd like to entertain me in a "proper" restaurant, but New Bedford's local chefs are all doing nouvelle cuisine. Allen doesn't forgive inedible garnishes; artsy combinations of weird tastes make his blood pressure rise. His face gets redder, the eyes bulge, and then, in true Yankee spirit, "Sweetheart, don't you know how awful it is when they top perfectly good garden carrots with pineapple puree?" This is the plantsman who, back in February, showed me a luscious, warm red azalea blooming in Greenhouse Number 5 when it was zero degrees outside, snow was banked up against the plastic walls, and I wished I had my sunglasses. But the azalea with the juicy color of a sun-ripened tomato, you couldn't miss it. "Now that's RED!" he said. "It's red the way nature meant red to be, as in a poppy or geranium. No blue in it. Too unnatural, inorganic." ✺ Forget he was honored by the American Horticultural Society as Nurseryman of the Year, and he's received so many silver bowls that people say he intimidates the judges. You know what he did with those bowls? He sold them to pay for his son's horticultural education. Don't tell him about composting. ✺ Yet I sense a rare moment of humility when this world-class gardener apologizes for never having been "to the Continent," saying it with the native New England accent that turns *o*'s into *ah*'s. Still apologizing, he imagines that the Continent is where the greatest garden designs are, but he's lost me. I'm looking around and mumbling about Giorgio Morandi, the Bolognese artist who hardly left his neighborhood, who kept reworking still lifes of the same old dusty accessories and now they're calling him the greatest Italian painter of the twentieth century. Way to go, Giorgio. 🌿 Eat with someone and you'll know if they're cooking, is what I say. 🌿 After dinner I cut across the nursery, because in the distance whole green-houses—long as city blocks—are packed with Allen Haskell's ultimate folly. Mine too. Although he wants you to think he began growing potted topiaries because it didn't pay to heat empty houses between seasons, I know better. After Allen has worked an eighteen-hour day, forgetting his weariness he will pick up a favorite pair of pruners and, probably with less thought than he gives to clipping his toenails, start grooming another rank of unkempt green sol-diers, each one standing tall and straight and waiting for its regimental haircut. 🌿 "At

"I like trees because they seem more resigned to the way th

times," he says, "I feel more like a barber." Tell me. Early in the morning, before the waterproofers on my terrace have juiced up their jackhammers, I'm out there pruning, trying the best I know how to shape a week that's cutting it close. 🌿 Right now I'm eyeballing lollipop heads of lavender, westringia, santolina, bay laurel, and rosemary plants in full flower, plus aisles and aisles of scented-leaf geraniums that smell like pepper, chocolate, or cinnamon when you brush against the leaves. But to me the most wondrous thing of all is that everything I see began right here, from nothing more horticulturally mumbo jumbo than taking a little cutting at the right time and rooting it in a pot of soil. And when *is* the right time? 🌿 Spring, they say, is usually the best season for transplanting. But if you really want to know, every seedling, rooting, plug tray, and young sapling, even grown-up stock like me, is somewhat set back when moved—before it gets going again. 🌿 When you're a city child with New York eyes you become street smart and subway wise, sure as a sewer rat on a couple of tokens. You get rooted

ave to live than other things do." (Willa Cather, "O Pioneers!" 1913)

by mastering underground routes; you develop sinewy muscle and merciful character, a strength through sensitivity. There's no place for hubris down there when they're packing more than fashion in baggy jeans. Riding those trains punctures the pompous, holds arrogance at bay. But years later, after the subterranean pathways had slipped my mind, it got me nervous to have misplaced my subway savvy. Even worse, I was haughty enough to mistake ignorance for independence. The Porsche, the Mercedes, and the speediest of all piston-powered twin-engine planes—maybe not the highest level of comfort in the cabin but faster than some turboprops and with room for the pilot, the husband, the wife, the friend, and the carrier with the cat—were all good ways to travel if you're missing direction. One day I preferred to walk. No driver or pilot could take me where I was going. My thoughts were earthbound, and I longed to return to that underworld equalizer. I was ready to come in for the landing. Preferring airborne things with feathered wings, I continued to see man and nature as one and still hadn't opened the manual on right-seat piloting. We were flying at maximum revolutions per minute, nose pointing straight down; the trip was on a collision course heading for disaster. Life had gotten too fast for feelings, devoid of details. Like the blast-off, it was accelerated and noisy, and what I wanted was silent scenery back in my vision. More than ever my weightless head was looping around in the clouds. I needed to be grounded, and the earth looks good when nature's best rainbow is an orgy of greens. Now, if I'm not taking the bus from Port Authority it's an eight-hour drive in a van, or a truck when I get a lift with Kevin. But at least I won't be coming out of a fog bank when we get off that highway and

"There is no gardening without humility. Nature is constantly sending even its oldest scholars to the bottom of the class for some egregious blunder."
(Alfred Austin, English poet Laureate, "The Garden That I Love," 1705)

"Who loves a garden Still his Eden keeps."
(Amos Bronson Alcott, "Tablets" 1868)

I see Eden down the road from the Shawmut Diner. ⚘ Allen Haskell's nursery is a limitless dream. The Puritan work ethic stirred with passion are the ingredients in his horticultural style. Just when you think the guy's gotten it all together, he's mouthing off about propagating a rare wild orchid from China. Or maybe you're wondering who originally bid $3,000 for Sir John Thouron's famous yellow clivia at the Arnold Arboretum Rare Plant Auction. Come back in a month and he's busy moving his whole hosta collection from one end of the place to the other. Nothing can stop Allen Haskell from doing it again if he can do it better. Imagine the gall to up and turn a mature *Cedrus atlantica* 'Glauca Pendula' after it'd been growing for about twenty years in one attitude because the original orientation of the weeping blue atlas cedar never looked right. The tree's made an amazing recovery, and know what? Allen was right. ⚘ One summer, many years ago, he and his staff dug a narrow trench through an area of the nursery where surface water just lay on the hardpan soil. Most people would dig a ditch, pour cement, then sit back with a beer. Allen Haskell carefully lined his narrow canal with cobblestones that were brought over to New Bedford as ballast on whaling ships and later used to pave the steeply pitched horse-trodden streets of nearby Fall River. The rough-cut stones are a beautiful and functional landscaping element, adding texture to the shimmering ribbon of water. But all the guy wanted was to show his grandson the principle of the new canal. They floated a leaf down the center and, little hand in big hand, raced it to the far end. ⚘ Then Allen Haskell took his Dewar's—chilled, no ice. He's a great horticulturist, I never said a saint. ⚘

"Remember that the most beautiful things in the world are the most useless; peacocks and lilies for instance." (John Ruskin, "The Stones of Venice," 1851-1853)

"Changing one's mind is a sign of strength." (Christopher Lloyd, "In My Garden," 1994)

Roots

I GARDEN IN TIGHT QUARTERS. ALWAYS HAVE AND PROBABLY always will. Everything I grow grows in a container, in an earthbound situation. Anyway, my dictionary reminds me that a garden is just a

"It's not too big, it's not too small, it's just right." (Goldilocks)

"collection of plants." Sure I meant when she said, "It about a little garden only wide!" in the slender summer-cottage garden off shire. Later on she says, "It work one can find to do in and I'm right there with Celia. to forget about taproots mortar joints, or not to worry wave and there's no sign of today's only Monday? I has over eleven miles of running tainer gardening is confining? through a cathedral of used to make a nave down before anyone ever heard of I'm lying under the limbs

know what Celia Thaxter seems strange to write a book 50 feet long by 15 feet volume describing her the coast of New Hamp- is wonderful how much so tiny a plot of ground," But wouldn't it be swell squirming through loose when we're having a heat rain 'til the weekend and mean, if one barley plant roots, don't you agree con- Or sometimes I'll be walking branches—the way they every Main Street in America Dutch elm disease—and next of a two-hundred-year-old

copper beech, reading about how in Roman times they built whole garden rooms right into trunk cavities. And know what? I'm getting j-e-a-l-o-u-s. There's something to be said for leafy canopies up there in cahoots with the clouds, and feeder roots with room enough to roam. Why, already I'm sleeping better, just knowing about how trees that size draw up water in the middle of the night and then flush it out to neighboring plants. ✻ In addition to scrounging the soil for moisture and dissolved nutrients, roots provide anchorage. They should be encouraged to grow deep, to reach down for their water, food, and stability. None of this "I'll just lie near the soil line and take a sip every now and then" business. Out there forces work overtime to unearth even mature trees and established gardens. Those with just a pretty face don't have a prayer. In spring, some quick  hit of chemical fertilizer produces a rush of greenery, and sure, things will look good for a while. But "face value" has none. Nitrogen-lush plants are fluff-heads, not to mention light-footed, when up against the odds. They've been forced to grow too fast on root systems that won't sustain them. ✻ Remember—Mother Nature will keep you and your garden going every month of the year, so what you're admiring better be able to tough out droughts, heat waves, and insect blights in summer, the persistent winds of fall's transitional storms and hurricanes, and the icy frosts and dangerous thaws of winter. Otherwise, just when you think the birds are ready to sing, a false spring can zap your blossom preemies. Yes, trees can throw out auxiliary buds, but they only have so much energy, which means that in the end less of it goes into root or twig growth. ✻ Beautiful gardens must be ethereal yet grounded, flexible yet resilient. ✻

"Plant your feet firmly on the ground, the better to jump into the air." (Joan Miró, 20ᵗʰ c. Spanish artist)

Diary of A Nest

AT DUSK OR AT DAWN, THAT'S WHEN THE AIR IS COOLEST. It's the perfect time for watering because the wet will soak way down when there's less evaporation. Also, if any drops get on the Boston ivy, there's no sun to burn the leaves. But these reasons aren't why I wait to water. It's neither night nor day when I snake rubber hoses between containerized trees. I'm in my gardens at twilight because the stillness magnifies the sorcery. It's the last Sunday in April, and a pair of visitors I never noticed before are sharing my world while taking me from it. One is at the top of my chimney where the brickwork ends and the sheet metal begins, and the mate is answering from a TV antenna across the street where the gardener I was having an affair with used to work. The duetting birds are singing extravagant songs, and with so much yodeling back and forth my eyes get caught in a thorny thicket. For weeks the broken twigs—curiously all about the same size—had been dropping in the sedum growing at the base of my fullest hawthorn, but it didn't mean anything to me. As with everything else out of whack up here, I blamed it on the wind. And the wind was strong that spring, but that part comes later. The next day the sun isn't even up, but I feel like a kid on Christmas morning. Except I'm a woman coming to see what's been under the tree all along. Gee whiz. What other wonders are missed when you can't translate the language? Because even in a city that reveres the rented Rolls Royce or a culture that gives celebrity status to

ten more explanatory than any description." (Wilfrid Blunt, "The Art of Botanical Illustration" 1950)

newly freed white-collar criminals, the enthralling grace of nature is still to be ferreted out. ❧ Mockingbirds, *Mimus polyglottos,* are "many-tongued mimics" and are among the several southerners that decided to stick around when the eating got good in the Northeast all year long. They like our city parks and our suburban backyards, and when they find other basics like water, cover, and nesting areas, there's no reason for migrating just to get out of the cold. They're putting up homes in tangled rose canes or anything else that will weave together for necessary shade and shelter. In case you didn't know—and I didn't before this all began—my hawthorn trees are in the rose family, Rosaceae. ❧ At one time hawthorns regularly flowered in May. Their blooming branches were a propitious omen—the end of winter and the beginning of spring, when crops were planted and birds built nests. Limbs, luscious with scented alabaster umbels,

" Enclose gardens with hedges made of roses or other thorny bushes."
(Petrus de Crescentius, "Opus Ruralium Commodorum," 1304-1309)

made the trees as fetching as nubile maidens. Blossomed boughs symbolized conjugal union, a flowering future. But like my taxus, hawthorns are *bois noble;* hardly the veiled appeal of ingenue brides. They grow to great age with remarkably durable wood. These are like the majestic ones—cherry, oak, and walnut; beech, elm, and ash— that stand for generations. 🌿 To a couple of mockingbirds who choose to live high above but nevertheless within the urban jungle, my hawthorns, with spiny limbs and berries from autumn through winter, with trunks thick as fruit trees outlining a would-be garth, must have seemed heavenly. 🌿 May 2: I'm too excited to sleep, and soon as I hear bird sounds I throw on one of my halfway outfits. I go upstairs and outside to see what's up. It's 4:00 A.M. and I wonder if nighttime means nothing to them. But over my head in the crotch of two limbs there's yesterday's find: the faint crosshatched beginnings of a nest that could easily double for crisscrossing hawthorn branches. The birds have already added prunings from my Boston ivy, *Parthenocissus tricuspidata* 'Vetchii', and dangling tendrils I'd cut off another vine, *Clematis terniflora,* the one with the bowers of white flowers in the fall, followed by silky seedheads. Maybe I'll never have to sweep again. 🌿 Wind is building up and, being it's a problem for me, I assume the same for them. Yet *they* chose this site—even with so much park right across the street so I tell myself, Relax. 🌿 May 3: It's very windy and I don't see or hear them. I'm telling everyone, "I told you so." 🌿 May 4: Today the winds have stopped and the air is filled with a chorus, like in the forest when the sun is rising. It could be a hundred birds out there, but I only see the two who are back and building a nest; I wonder which song is actually theirs. I load my new camera and hope I did it right because I really want that picture, the one with the bird working the nest from the inside. I think it's the female. She fusses over every piece of twig, and then for a real bit of refinement she presses her roly-poly body against the sides and, after that, on two of the skinniest legs you ever saw, she jumps up and down in the middle. I guess to compact the bottom, because that's what I do when I've got all the prunings together on the ground and I want to flatten the bundle. ⚘ But every now and then the other bird gets inside the nest and uses the top of his beak to nudge things that maybe she overlooked, which reminds me of the way my cat, Timothy, pushes my arm with the top of his head when he's giving the orders. ⚘ They're using shorter twigs now, and it's a good idea since the nest still looks pretty airy. Besides, the longer branches kept getting caught in her feathers or lodged in the thorns so they had to shake everything like crazy to get it loose, which made me worry that the only thing coming apart would be the nest they're building. By the time I'm watering at twilight, I'm not just imagining progress. ⚘ May 5: It's pouring rain. They tried working when it was only drizzling, but except for hearing their sounds, I can't really say I saw any activity. Where do they go in this kind of weather? ⚘ May 6: Clear parts of sky are coming through on the horizon even though things are sopping wet. Twigs are dripping down from the nest and it looks exactly like when riggers are working up here, cables and ropes hanging over the sides of the building. The birds are back and working on their

"If you please yourself, you know you've pleased one person in the world." (Christopher Lloyd, 20th c. plantsman who writes about his celebrated gardens at Great Dixter) in East Sussex)

very soggy nest. 🌿 CMay 7: It's windy but sunny. They must be up to the lining because they're picking from my trough with the *Antennaria dioica;* the common name, cat's paw, is exactly the way this dwarf carpeting plant feels. He's bringing the silvery green tufts back to her in beakfuls—imagine, whole beakfuls—all tangled up and matted from the wind and rain. She's been trying to pull it apart for nearly an hour; it's worse than a knot in a necklace. Finally she flies the mess over to the parapet wall where she can work on surer footing. You show him, girl! 🌿 Fred, who knows about birds, said I should put out some raisins, eggshells, and water. Isn't it interesting about life how someone always pops up with information just when you need it? 🌿 May 8: It's 45 degrees: overcast, cold, and very windy. She grabs a raisin like she's doing something criminal, and flies off somewhere else to eat it. 🌿 CMay 9: The day is bright, sunny, and warmish. I love the way they added the hawthorn branch with the leaves so now it's really like a bluff. I wonder if that's where the Pomo Indians got the idea of weaving their baskets with the feathers. I also see a bit of juniper and a piece of white string, which I guess they liked better than the angora I put out for them when Fred also told me to leave some yarn around. The photos I took the other day came out great. It's good I didn't waste time reading the instructions. 🌿 I love seeing them snitch a raisin, which now I'm serving in a grapefruit half, but the other day when one got stuck on his beak it got both of us nervous. She's spending more and more time hanging around the nest. 🌿 May 10: The whole day it's been pouring. The grapefruit shell collects water better than my rain meter. I haven't seen them or heard any bird sounds; I hope they're okay. I wonder how much repair work will have to be done, even though no time was wasted fixing things up after the last storm. These guys certainly aren't like beavers, who look at dam maintenance and upkeep as everyday routine. 🍃 *May 11:* Today it's rainy, cold, windy, and misty. The weather won't give in. I picked up the grapefruit that blew over last night and put fresh raisins in it with new eggshells, even though I never see the birds go for the egg-shells. All of a sudden, from out of I-don't-know-where, one of them stabs a raisin and flies away. 🍃 *May 12:* The sky is clearing. After two days of pouring rain I go outside to look around. They didn't touch the eggshells, but all the raisins are gone. The two of them are sitting on the parapet wall, every eye on the architecture. Then one of them makes a shrilling sound like I never heard before. At about 6:30 P.M. I unroll the hoses and start to water. That's when I see her in the nest, not standing but sitting. Her head is facing out and her tail is looking up. I water for over an hour and all that time he's rid-ing shotgun on the chimney flue. If he suspects trouble he gives a whistle, and that's when she scrunches down and takes her tail with her. 🍃 *May 17:* At about 11:00 A.M. the sun comes out. The rain has poured for two solid days, and they haven't stopped eating the new batch of raisins. Unless it's my imagination, the birds look thinner. She's been sitting on the nest since Friday or Saturday, through all the rain-and-wind storms. I wonder if there will be chicks by

"There's nothing he doesn't know—the cat on the stove." (Fusei, 20th c. haiku poet)

Sunday—Mother's Day. Tonight Timothy finally caught on and he's screaming like a prisoner, just denied parole. Me, I finally got a bird book. It says the female mockingbird incubates the eggs for twelve days. May 24: It's very rainy, and they look so pathetic when they're wet like this. She came down for the raisins I'd just put out, but she had trouble taking off and stopped on several branches while going back up. Her feathers are matted and soggy, which must be the same as schlepping an extra carryon. May 28: They make a terrible warning cry when they see Timothy, even though he's inside and sleeping most of the time. They're still eating the raisins, but this afternoon one of them was toting a bug back to the nest in its beak. Memorial Day, May 29: Today I got on top of the tall ladder and what I saw were two wide-open mouths. The book says a clutch of mockingbirds usually averages four. There I was, looking right down their throats, and the parents didn't say boo. Is anybody home? May 31: From my desk where I'm working I can make out baby birds peeking from the top of the nest—plain as the moth in her beak she brought back for a meal. June 3: My birds have become very antisocial. They're diving at me—right at my head—every time I'm anywhere near the nest. It's actually scary. Now I don't even put the hose back on the holder under the tree when I get through watering. June 5: The nestlings are reaching up with skinny little necks and squeaky voices—much louder than before—and from what I can tell, their bodies are larger and sturdier. 🌿 **June 8:** This morning the sky was so clear and blue I should have known the heavens were covering up for something. Last night was one of the worst rainstorms I ever remember, the kind where the next day you wake up and everything is different. You know that kind of storm? A storm that changes everything. When whatever happened before is going to be different now. In the afternoon I put out more raisins under the tree and that's when I saw the little bird in the sedum, all wet and stringy. Another was lying on top of the hose that I left unrolled in the middle of the terrace. That one was probably trying to get away, trying to fly for the first time. Trying to fly for the first time in the storm that was one of the worst storms I ever remember. I found the other two birds between the planter and the wall. 🌿 The problem with that spring was the flowers weren't opening. There was so little sun, just days and days of rain. Yet right after that last storm, the last one for the fledglings, the park looked green and lush. It was as voluptuous as color could get. Treetops became emerald puffs of clouds, dropped from the sky. My hawthorns finally had veils of white, and the marguerite daisies also decided to open. There were masses and masses of tiny blossoms on the fraises des bois, which meant I would have a big crop in June. But without the birds none of it mattered. My garden felt like the most barren place on earth. 🌿

The Gardener asked "Who plucked this flower?" The master said, "I plucked it for Myself," and the Gardener held his peace.
(Epitaph on a child's gravestone in Sellack Churchyard, Herefordshire)

"Not only the days but life itself lengthens in summer

Richard Jefferies, "The Pageant of Summer," 1905)

"Every day I've lived I wanted to flower more and more." (Louise Nevelson, American Sculptor 1900-1988)

Summer

IN THE FOLLOWING WEEKS FIELDS WILL BLOOM with the Greek prefix for "sun," like *heliopsis,* and of course the eternal symbol of constancy, *Helianthus annuus,* our own North American native, the annual sunflower. Flowers with golden rays for petals mirror the giver of light and life. Herbs and blossoms of radiant form—chamomile, rudbeckia, even weedy dandelions, pop up in the garden, behind the garage, along the highways, at the bus stops. But what better suggests the central body of the solar system than the modest daisy? With a collar of petals that closes at night or if it starts to rain, daisies are from the Old English *daeges eage,* the "day's eye." ✺ Hooray for the longest days of the year when the sun graces more than the sky. ✺ Yet in the middle of July, on the top of a roof when it's hot like this, all I'm thinking is, Why bother rewinding hoses if I'll be watering again at twilight? Native Americans knew to call this month the Thunder Moon: Summer is in full swing and gardens need a drink now. Rain-dancing might help, but it's been 90 degrees or above for eleven of the past twelve days, and Nobody Beats the Wiz says they're moving 250 air conditioners a week at Avenue U in Brooklyn, up from the usual 75 when it's just plain hot. I hear there's an ozone alert, the humidity is a killer, and even though meteorologists say we've seen worse summers, this one must be breaking some kind of record. The dew point—buzzword for

"Flowers

* The month is on track for becoming the driest since the Federal Government began recording monthly rainfall in Central Park in 1869." ("The New York Times," August 24, 1995)

"absolute moisture in the air"—can't seem to come down. Psst . . . in gardener-speak, we've got the kind of weather that's fine for fungus.

My plants right now remind me of Timothy, snoozing over there on the tile floor behind the toilet bowl where it's dripping. With all due respect to felines, these are dog days, when the canine star, Sirius—from *Seirios,* "the scorcher"—two times the mass and twice the diameter of the sun, will do anything for attention. In periods of combined heat and very little rain, catnapping's not a bad idea. Plants need to conserve energy; they're not looking for food, so— except for your tropicals—forget about feeding. Fresh green growth will only make them more enticing to insects, and we want to reduce the stress they're already under. Putting out toxins to repel natural enemies is not a priority when something's dying of thirst.

"July: This month bears the highest record for heat of any this summer." (Edith Holden, "The Country Diary of an Edwardian Lady," 1906)

"are the stars of the earth" (Pierre-Joseph Redouté, Botanical artist, 1759-1840)

For a gardener who loves to water everything by hand, I'm embarrassed to say automatic watering systems with little PVC drip-tubes that spaghetti over the flower beds with irrigation nozzles prone to clogging are looking better the longer it doesn't rain. But nowadays everything's hooked up to a timer and whole yards are on automatic pilot, so pretty soon we're seeing more electronic props than plants. Maybe you like the noise of smelly, dirty, polluting, heavy-to-use power tools. I love the scratchy sound from the tines of a classic bamboo rake. I'd rather listen to birdsong than a motorized leaf-blower. ⅋ Hey, all I'm saying is I want a little time off. I'm stressed out, way behind schedule, and about to forget that carrying water to the gods was once a noble occupation. ⅋ Three quarters of the Earth's surface is covered by water. If all the lands were leveled, water would cover everything to a depth of over two miles. From the beginning of time when the four rivers of life crisscrossed the Garden of Eden, nothing ever defined and designed gardens more than the availability of water. Remember the way ancient Persians in the desert planted lush oases behind walls and around axial ponds so all the flowers and trees were never far from irrigation? Or how the American Indians in the Southwest grew their corn, beans, and squash at the bottoms of canyons because they figured reserves of moisture lay beneath the surface in the seasonally dry streams? ⅋ And then you have Versailles, with a bad case of fountain-envy. Louis XIV ordered that his father's little hunting lodge be transformed into a palace fit for a monarch before he gave himself the moniker "Sun King" and

Sunflowers *are the original Sunworshippers.*

long before we spoke in sound bites. He wanted waterfalls, formal cascades, ornamental canals, jets, runnels, and grottoes that would outdo Italy, where gravity was good and water was second nature. No matter that France was flat and lacked natural springs. Advances in hydraulics were supposed to engineer tributaries from the Seine into huge pumping stations, then over to aqueducts and finally to Versailles's fourteen hundred fountains. But imagine, even after all that they didn't have what it takes. (Kind of like my problems with the flushometers in a penthouse: the address sounds posh, but there's never enough water pressure.) Only when the king and his guests were touring the grounds could they pull out all the stops, have every geyser going at once. ✺ The natural landscape that became the formal gardens of seventeenth-century France is gardening metaphor, a powerful person's attempt to strong-arm Mother Nature. It's horti-culture as a means to an end, and it's still going on today. On east-ern Long Island, where the soil is mostly sand, bowling greens of the finest baize turf—the kind that grow so well where there's good rainfall and look so right in England when they're mowed in stripes—have become prerequisite garden one-upmanship for beachfront estates. Your status is measured by the size of your lawn. ✺ When Alfonso tells me his father always planted and sowed according to the phases of the moon, it's not some old wives' tale. Every organism, every little seed in your garden, needs water. And because lunar rhythms have an effect on the Earth's magnetic field, which in turn acts on growth, in the end the garden will respond in tides like the sea. ✺

"I do not envy the owners of very large gardens. The garden should fit its master or his tastes, just as his clothes do; it should be neither too large nor too small, but just comfortable."
(Gertrude Jekyll, "Wood and Garden," 1899)

"A lawn is nature under culture's boot."
(Michael Pollan, "Second Nature," 1991)

They follow the rays in slow motion.

Sharing

EVER WONDER WHAT MAKES GARDENERS SO BIG-HEARTED?
Try complimenting the zucchini. Say my fraises des bois are as good
as the ones you ate in the South of France. Or mention something
about the rosemary topiaries, like by the way how much greener they
look ever since the spider mites are gone. Next thing you're going
home toting a doggy bag with one of everything. ✌ Are gardeners simply handing out cigars because those seeds they planted
sprouted in twenty-

eight days the way the packet said they would, and now all those babies need homes? ✿ To garden is to share. You pass along a plant, a cutting, some seeds, some seedlings, a division, and it's like waiting to see how the recipe comes out when someone else is cooking. I gave a bush of Russian sage, *Perovskia atriplicifolia,* to my doorman Alfonso, but it was too big for his fire escape so he planted it in his sister's garden. That was before the rest of my Russian sage died over the winter—but I knew where to go for some divisions. Jen calls it making a backup disk on the computer. ✿ Or, as Annie Dillard explains in her book *The Writing Life:* "One of the few things I know about writing is this: spend it all, shoot it, play it, lose it, all right away, every time. Do not hoard what seems good for a later place in the book, or for another book; give it, give it all, give it now. . . .

Something more will arise for later, something better. These things fill from behind, from beneath, like well water. Similarly, the impulse to keep to yourself what you have learned is not only shameful, it is destructive. Anything you do not give freely and abundantly becomes lost to you.

"Plant your seeds in a row, one for the pheasant, one for the crow, one to eat and one to grow."
(Traditional rhyme)

"Too much of a good thing can be wonderful."
(Mae West)

You open your safe and find ashes." Lilibeth, someone I work with, needed a Christmas tree stand, so I told her that in this neck of the woods they chuck the tree and everything, which is another way of saying I'm sure we'll find one downstairs after the holidays. Alfonso hears this and thinks he still has the extra one from last year on the top shelf of his closet, along with the brand-new baby outfits he found in the back hall. The grandfather who's chief of the village in Mali where I sponsor a child says his people think it's "dead white-man's clothes" they're sending over when coats and jackets are still good enough to wear. That afternoon Alfonso walks in with last year's stand for Lilibeth—in the original carton, if you please—plus the lucky stiff also found a new terra rosa pot someone just threw out. Maybe because the rim was chipped. It's a nice flat one, he says, and he wants me to have it because my shallow-rooted semper-vivum are going to love it. The snow was coming down hard when we put the pot outside, hoping the weather would also make an impression. The next morning, at a quarter to six, I'm on my way to the pool. When I get back Alfonso is still on his doorman shift, looking like he just won the fifth race at Aqueduct; he holds up another Christmas tree stand he found outside on the curb, and it's not even Christmas yet. Last winter when all my topiaries had spider mites, of course that was when the New York Botanical Garden invited me to design a garden setting at their place for June. They'd feature my first book, the one on growing topiaries, and there would be a signing, and if I was lucky some fans

Foxgloves are also called "fairy folk gloves," "witch's bells," "finger flowers."

and "fairy thimbles"

besides my mother, Diane, and Janee—relatives and friends don't count—would show up. I'm thinking, Abbie, you turn this down and the Washington Arboretum crosses you off their list. So that's why one day in early spring I'm in the flower market on Twenty-eighth Street—in the gutter—scrunched between trucks filled with fresh-cut stems from the Netherlands. (I remember the first time I went to Holland, I wanted to see those flower auctions in Aalsmeer with the big clock on the wall even more than Rembrandt's studio.) I'm sitting on an upside-down flower bucket drawing pots of digitalis because Kevin just got some good ones in for Easter. But from where I'm perched, eye level with the garbage, I see a bunch of leftover Allen Haskell topiaries hiding in the back of the shop, and to be honest they looked as bad as mine. ✳ "Kevin," I said, "could I borrow those plants, get a little life in them, use them for my display, then I'll return them?" ✳ I gave them love, attention, and a good eastern exposure. By show time they were gorgeous, and by the time they went back to Kevin in September some of them were even blooming. ✳ Sharing is nothing more than recycling, and gardeners have been at it long before there was a logo. Something dies up here and a bunch of pots get repositioned. If anyone wants to know how I design my garden, I swear I let the plants tell me what to do. ✳ Remember? I work best with leftovers. I'm against building new architecture and I've never had children because I'd rather save what's out there already. I finish last night's dessert for breakfast, and the vests I sew from my ravel-sleeved sweatshirts made sense even before Armani did "grunge." If yes-

"Depending on location and available resources there are many ways of reaching your idealized garden. If it works for you—it works."
("Gardening Tips from the National Trust," 1994)

"Most ideas come after you start working—not before."
(Tom Paxton, folksinger & songwriter, 1995)

terday's newspaper is what I need, or suppose I'm in a hurry for an empty mayonnaise jar to hold the remaining paint which I'll probably never use since I'm already thinking of changing the color, I'm the tenant who shops the basement of our fancy-schmancy apartment building because the way I see it, our recycling room is the local dump. Maybe it comes from watching all those squirrels in the park burying their nuts and acorns in the fall. Does anyone really think squirrels are able to keep track of where they're hiding everything, so come spring they can say, Oh no, that's mine—yours is over there? If someone says "log it" to a beaver, does the beaver open his Filofax and start writing? It's more like he joins the colony of flat-tailed, five-toed forepawed, webbed hind-footed-lumberjacks with sharp teeth and starts sizing up the nearest

"There is no enough in nature." (Richard Jefferies, 19th c.

tree. I suspect the company policy is every critter works her shift, holds up her end of the deal, then when payday comes it's share and share alike. Squirrels aren't nickel-and-diming each other. None of this "one for you, one for me" business. What they don't eat—what's left over—becomes the tree they share with us; they don't give a hoot about overplanting. There's no government paying them to curb it with the acorns. ✹ And that tree, in addition to its beauty, absorbs pollutants, improves water quality, abates noise, and offers pro- tection and shade, as well as providing nesting sites for squirrels and all the other guys. Phew. In the forest, trees are among the largest and longest lived organisms. But in New York City, up to twenty thousand trees die annually. Maybe it's good to keep in mind that larger, older trees remove sixty to seventy times more pollution than newly planted saplings. Maybe you should also know that when someone hurts a city tree, they're liable for the amount of wood the tree contained, according to Article 1, Section 4, of the City of New York Parks and Recreation Department's rules and regulations. In other words, if the victim had a 20-inch diameter, the perp owes twenty-five new trees, 4 inches across. ✹ As the announcer says when the mike gets passed, "Over to you." ✹

English writer)

" Hurt not the earth,
neither the Sea,
nor the trees."
(Revelation 7: 13)

Seats

DO I JUST LIKE GARDENS BECAUSE THEY'RE ONE MORE ROOM TO furnish? The way I used to think a baby sister or even a baby brother would be another doll to dress? ✌ Truth is, I'm not big on bedroom suites, and if you really want to know how I live, all that's in my living room is a couch to sit on and some tables, and the tables are where the books sit. I wish they'd stop sending me catalogues full of outdoor furniture when I've got the best seat in the house. ✌ Whether civilizations gardened for pleasure or provisions, the plot always featured a place to rest and regroup. Back in the 1200s, when herbs were grown in cloistered patterns so the ones that could kill you were over there and the ones that dyed the cloth were in the patch of plants over here, Albertus Magnus, the thirteenth-century Dominican theologian and scientist, wrote the treatise *On Vegetables and Plants.* Sure enough, his instructions on arranging a pleasure garden advised, "There should be a bench of flowering turf." Flowers meant for sitting on? No "Keep Off the Grass" signs? Dark Ages? ✌ From the downy softness of the chamomile seat at Sissinghurst to the robust beauty of Roberto Burle Marx's granite boulders in a Brazilian rain forest, the most successful seats create a soothing balance between

"A garden without seats is unfriendly." (Christopher Lloyd, "In My Garden," 1994)

nature and the human touch. ⚘ Garden seats have been made from sod, wood, wicker, stone, and iron both wrought and cast. And now? Get cozy in the fin de siècle accomplishment of twentieth-century gardening, polypropylene. ⚘ But this isn't about portable deck chairs or foldaway furniture. A proper garden seat should be rooted in the greenery. It's a permanent and appropriate feature, not a pit stop. If you're thinking that any old crate will do, remember how careful you were about where the swimming pool went? Or maybe it was the sundial. Or the *Magnolia grandiflora* you planted the day your daughter was born. The right perch is a welcome invitation, suggesting comfort, ease, and a time to pause. That's why Gertrude Jekyll said, "It rests the eye as well as the body." ⚘ I've been canoeing and hiking all morning in the High Peaks of the Adirondacks, the only virgin forest left in the Northeast, and I'm ready for lunch. And because this national park was deemed "forever wild" under the state constitution over one hundred years ago, there are plenty of reserved seats. I choose a moss-covered toppled tree, timber that will never be logged again, and my legs are stretched out in the lush splendor of primeval ferns with my back and shoulders up against the big flat rock that's warm from the morning sun. I should bless the peanut-butter-and-jelly sandwiches because nothing tastes better in the woods, but how about we all say grace for a group of environmentalists who understood that land like this had to be set aside and protected if it

"The forests and mountains and desert canyons are holier than our churches. Therefore let us behave accordingly." (Edward Abbey, radical environmentalist who died in 1989)

Lunch break at Elk Lake, autumnal equinox, 1994

was ever to recover from the voracious logging of the 1800s. 🌿 Or there I am, it's a hot day in a Roman garden with endless blue sky and no clouds for relief, and nothing looks or feels better against the backs of bare thighs than the cool, soothing slab of finely carved Carrara marble at the base of the fountain where the water has been dribbling for so long that a little stream is cutting through the stone. 🌿 But this same gorgeous marble seat on Nantucket Island, where the evening air gives you goose bumps in July? I'll take a teak bench sanded and grayed by sea spray when I'm watching shooting stars "in gardens of lesser preten- sions," as Ger- trude Jekyll also said. 🌿 Not every seat is right for every site. 🌿 Remember the spring when the crown prince of Japan was introducing his betrothed, the new Chrysanthe- mum Princess? She was the gal of whom everyone thought, If she's so contemporary, why give it all up to sit on a throne? I thought, Why's the royal couple on the front page of the *New York Times* sitting in palace gardens on a pair of webbed alu- minum numbers? The kind on sale outside Home Depot along with the rinky-dink lawn chaises in turquoise. Was this a nod to democ- racy? Were they saying we're all salt of the earth when it comes to the soil? Especially when the royal garden seat—probably some outra- geous treasure and certainly a more honest expression of an oriental garden tradition—was behind those imperial evergreens wondering

My thinking went, If it's in pellet form—dissolved only during watering, absorbed just through the roots—I'll get those no-goods from the inside out without disturbing the air. But they don't call them "systemics" for nothing. The chemical moves through the sap, affecting the entire system from feeder roots finer than eyelash hairs to the tip of every bud. Doesn't distinguish between ladybugs and bad bugs. That's why, halfway through July, I wondered about the birdsong. I wasn't hearing any up here. ✭ I can only speak for myself but I always had—and still have—trouble following instructions. I do better with show-and-tell. I honestly don't remember where it was written "Birds and other wildlife in treated areas may be killed" on the label. On top of that, I also suffer from the grass-is-greener-some-where-else syndrome, so maybe I was thinking somewhere else was where the real birds were. ✭ But all birds indicate the amount of protection or disturbance in an area. Long Island used to be home to the largest osprey population in the Northeast. That was before DDT caused calcium deficiency in their eggs, making them too fragile to incubate. Or before real-estate development along shorelines reduced stands of tall trees overlooking open water, the preferred nesting sites of these majestic winged creatures. A bird's presence or absence becomes a signal that's easy to see and hear. They're telling us if habitats are okay: Whether the water is polluted and perhaps there aren't enough herrings in the sea for the penguins in the Antarctic, or maybe that the red-tailed hawks have returned to Central Park because it's filled with rats, or that my hawthorn trees were bloated with systemic. Like butterflies—a mere dip in light from a passing cloud causes their wings to close—birds are highly sensitive strobes of the woodlands and wetlands, as well as of city life. 🌿 When I was eight, every kid on the block came out at twilight because musical insects were turning up the volume and hocus pocus was in the air. There would be crooning crickets, a racket of grasshoppers, and the shrill of katydids up in the trees, which I still think sounds like a construction yard when they're building a house and using chain saws—not something you'd hear in nature. After dinner we'd hang out, holding our washed-out jelly jars, the screw-on lids punctured with holes from a big fat nail, ready to catch summer sky in a glass because fireflies were everywhere and the air was radiating right down to the ground. But the next day when yucky stuff was all that was left in the bottom of my jar, I thought it was wrong to turn out firefly lights. "Even the smallest of creatures carries a sun in its eye," it says on the bulletin board in the church where I swim. 🌿 Some years ago, before I was swimming at the church, a swarm of bees was zizzing around my spiral juniper with enough combined muscle to drag the needly branches downward. It looked like a black cloud and I wasn't humming along. 🌿 In the country, a bare-handed beekeeper will pay you to collect the colony with the queen in tow. But I'd already made several phone calls and, except for one guy who'd go in and get 'em for seventy-five bucks, it seemed city exterminators stick to bigger game. Roachy things. 🌿 This was before I understood that these beings are a gardener's gift from heaven. In *A Book of Bees,* Sue Hubbell, a commercial beekeeper and favorite nature writer, says she "gives each farmer a gallon of honey as rent every year for the privilege [of tending hives on their lands], but they

"Burning so easily,
extinguished so easily—
the firefly."
(Chine, haiku death
poem, 17th c.)

get much more from the bees themselves: luxuriant clover, abundant fruit and vegetable gardens, and dazzling flowerbeds." No one I knew ever knew things like that. 🌿 No one ever told me swarms are not particularly territorial about temporary locations; in fact, they're rather docile while waiting it out for scouts to find another home. If left to their own devices, the bees would have been up and away in twenty-four hours or so. It's that here-today-gone-tomorrow stuff that's always happening in nature. 🌿 I unrolled the fifty feet of rubber hose. Yet my ambivalent side convinced someone else to be the bully and shoot the bees. With direct streams of water at a pressure of 50 pounds per square inch, I was sure they'd swarm away in a huff. They stood their air space—kamikaze pilots on a mission of mercy, protectively veiling their queen. In less time than it takes to prune a rosebush, masses and masses of little workers who did what they had to do and have gone about their assignments in quiet ways since the beginning of time lay all over in heaps, like the ashen remains of a forest fire casting black shadows of death. 🌿 Hours later the katydids were still awake, but it's the dead and dying bees that wouldn't let me sleep. I kept going back upstairs to see what I'd done and, ultimately, what I'd lost. All night long under a dark sky—dark the way it used to be after the fireflies went out—I continued to sweep up the tragic remains of complex little creatures, some of them still twitching their furred feet hoping to kick this thing called death. 🌿 Nowadays my insect repellent is "eau de garlic." Next to the sins of Exxon's Valdez oil spill, it doesn't take much for an amateur environmentalist to think well of herself. 🌿

Ethics must be the aesthetics of the future." (Laurie Anderson, 20th c. Performance artist)

"My advice to the garden clubs of our land is to raise more hell and few

Jerry's dahlia fields, late September '94

ahlias." (William Allen White, Kansas newspaperman & 1923 Pulitzer winner)

AUTUMN

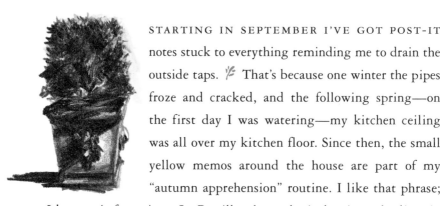

"Fall is the busiest time
for a Successful
gardener."
("Green-up Times," The
New York Botanical Garden
newsletter, 1994)

STARTING IN SEPTEMBER I'VE GOT POST-IT notes stuck to everything reminding me to drain the outside taps. ✳ That's because one winter the pipes froze and cracked, and the following spring—on the first day I was watering—my kitchen ceiling was all over my kitchen floor. Since then, the small yellow memos around the house are part of my "autumn apprehension" routine. I like that phrase; I borrow it from Anne La Bastille, the ecological writer who lives in the Adirondacks, and also says, "Summer arrives on July 4 and departs the day after." ✳ But with pollen still scattered on petals, who am I to close down a garden if a bee with drab yellow hair, shopworn as an old pigeon's feathers, keeps working the last of the morning glories? And when my terrace feels warmer than any room inside— the way the water in the pool where I swim is more inviting than the air—I'm praying the albino berries will ripen even though I'm losing sunlight faster than a plumbing main leaking water. ✳ I know I'm behaving like a child at this time of year, giving all kinds of excuses for staying out late, but yesterday it was balmy and rain was backing up nicely around the drains. So I grabbed the orchids and the topiaries I'd hate anything to happen to for one last drag on city smog and the kind of soaking they'll be missing for the next six months. I left them standing in the downpour all night long because I do better with a bit of anxiety in my life. ✳ In the morning when I opened the

door it felt humid and warm, more like Miami, and everything green was beaming. The sun wasn't up but already it was 68 degrees. Tell me I was lucky. Those plants and I have been together longer than a lot of my other relationships. Is this any way to treat friends? If the temperature had dropped in the middle of the night, all my work would have gone kaput. Worse still, without a hard-hat crew around, who else could I blame? At Château Petrus they'll often wait weeks after surrounding vineyards until someone gives the go-ahead to seize the moment and pick the grapes. That wine, in a class by itself, might sell for $600 a bottle—if you can find it. In a good year Petrus only produces four thousand cases, say compared to Château Margaux's forty thousand. But when the sun remains kind after a hot and dry summer, the fruit is left to cook on the vine, developing more alcohol with a higher sugar content. Which in the end

"Houseplants have become so firmly entrenched in the North American scene that they are rarely given a second thought." (Tovah Martin, "Once Upon a Windowsill," 1988)

"You can count the number of apples on one tree, but you can never

could make Château Petrus right on the money—if it doesn't rain. But fall is notoriously uncooperative in Bordeaux, and what might have been the vintage of the century could also become diluted juice because of a failed gamble. ✤ A guy I knew raised dahlias, one of the last local perennials of the season for New York's cut-flower market. If you ask me, they're more work than beauty, even if a field of them is really a picture. He grew coral ones and magenta ones, scarlet, crimson, red, violet, sulfur yellow, henna brown, and copper-orange striped ones. Then he had a row or two of whites just for me because they're my birthday flower, and you can keep all the other colors as far as I'm concerned. Given the right conditions, one dahlia plant is good for over sixty blooms, so about now he would turn the outdoor sprinklers on overnight to prevent a premature frost from blackening the heads and totally destroying his crop. The season is always too short for a flower seven months in the making. ✤ It's a clear-sky day and I'm walking through Central Park, where gray squirrels of wondrous grace, balanced by downy, white-edged tails, leap from limb to limb. If they weren't so common, we'd probably give these agile critters more respect. But they're all over the place, scratching earth, digging holes, and burying winter inventory. When I leave the park I see one taking his acorn and jumping into a window box while this other squirrel is heading for the bushes in front of my building with a six-pack of cheese crackers—the ones with the

count the number of trees in one apple," says an old proverb.

peanut-butter filling. ❧ While we humans are busy trying to outwit Mother Nature, I wonder if all this squirrel activity means it's going to be one helluva winter. Stockpiling makes sense in the woods, but here in the city? Wildlife is never far from a pretzel vendor, and litter baskets are open twenty-four hours a day. ❧ Sooner or later I give up. I start living the fall. I'm munching the Ida Red apple that Timothy's friend Aunt Sally gave me for my birthday and, after months of salad days, I'm thinking about making a stew. With just vegetables maybe. Little green bunions of brussels sprouts, so appealing when they're bite size and still on the stalk—not the starchy variety in cardboard cartons later on—are giving me ideas. ❧ Next I'm drilling windows in a gourd, the color of Granny Smith apples, that I picked up when they were taking down the decorations at the Fall Antiques Show at the Armory. I got the idea after I saw a dozen birdhouse gourds—or maybe they were feeders—hanging from the tree with leafless limbs in a rural hamlet in the South. It was when I was on my way to a forest of Oyamel firs in the Sierra Madres, the winter kingdom for millions of monarch butterflies, and I was going via Georgia because the largest freeflight, glass-enclosed conservatory in North America, the Cecil B. Day Butterfly Center, is something I also wanted to see. "If I ever find the right gourd I'm going to make a house like that," I used to tell Timothy, being that my cat stays on top of whatever I'm doing. I can hardly wait for the next antiques show. I make no apologies for the way I come by produce:

Upper room with a view...

and a peek-a-boo window for baby birds

Luxury duplex: I build to suit...

Mexico were impressed by roof gardens of the Aztecs." (Anthony

invading the Spaniards, and as at Pompeii, had them, Romans the ancient suspect in

I don't live by the farm. Besides, in this city, for better or worse, everything comes to you. ✐ I know it's autumn when I'm thinking thoughts of home. Even Timothy has moved back to the hearth, his winter residence by the stove that's a whisker away from the garbage bags. At least now he's in the right room if something I'm peeling or chopping falls on the floor. I welcome the different kind of energy I get from doing things indoors. The tools have been cleaned with gritty pads dunked in linseed oil and paint thinner, and the brushes and brooms are soaking over there in pails of water or else the bristles will be good for nothing but kindling. ✐ I've thought about forcing some minor bulbs. But if I'm feeling cabin-feverish later on, I'll buy ready-made pots of paperwhite narcissus, and if I'm also feeling flush I'll pick them up in February at the glamour-puss deli around the corner—the "convenience store." Because today I'm more interested in the *Sansevieria cylindrica.* Remember my green spiky specimen that the silicone crew tried to kill? I left it on the terrace for the rest of the summer, scarred and struggling in their faces—or maybe I wasn't ready to trash a plant known for long life in hard situations. Before I took it in last week I sliced off several husks, as if they were spears of asparagus. They had the look of survivors, so I shoved them into a mixture of sandy soil. I buttressed the stocky, leathery cuttings with stones because even if they'll produce rhizomatous shoots below the ground the way they're supposed to, right now there are no roots for support, and of course I can never find the rooting hormone powder when I need it. I thought about putting the remains of the original plant in the back hall when they collect the garbage tomorrow. But two weeks later it was still on my sill, and that's when I saw the shoot

Huxley, "Encyclopedia of Gardening," 1981)

that was pale green and thin, and—like Phoenix—elbowing its ways through the ashes. In a few days that spike will be in flower. Wanna know why I garden? ✳ Northeast winds are gusting to 40 miles an hour, and stuff is blowing around up here like tumbleweed because I was too busy with unripe berries to anchor anything down. I heard it might go to freezing tonight; I should check my *Farmer's Almanac,* but rain on the windows sounds like sleet, and I trust the doormen— or old-time New York City cabdrivers—when it comes to local weather. This morning before it got breezy I was out there peeking at the hawthorn trees, the row of hornbeams, and the taxus, and there are buds setting up for next spring so maybe it's about time for cerebral gardening. In just a minute I'll be disconnecting the hoses, draining the pipes, and turning the taps.

"Failure is the root of every Success." (Issey Miyake, fashion designer, 1994)

"Thank heavens, the sun has gone in, and I don't have to go out and enjoy it." (Logan Pearsall Smith, "Afterthoughts," 1931)

(We may think of gardens on housetops as a ver

90

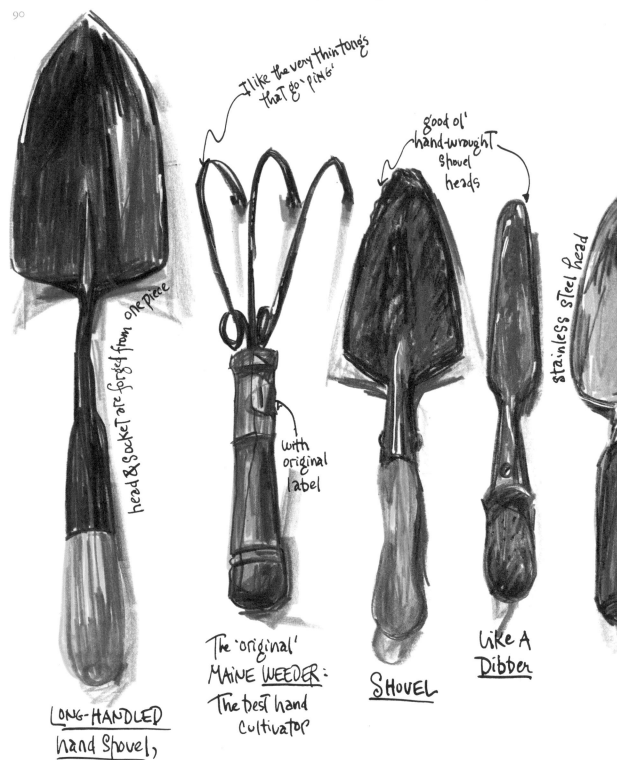

I like the very thin tongs that go "ping"

good ol' hand-wrought shovel heads

head & socket are forged from one piece

with original label

stainless steel head

LONG-HANDLED hand shovel, with hardwood handle (14½" overall)

The "original" MAINE WEEDER: The best hand cultivator

SHOVEL

Like A Dibber

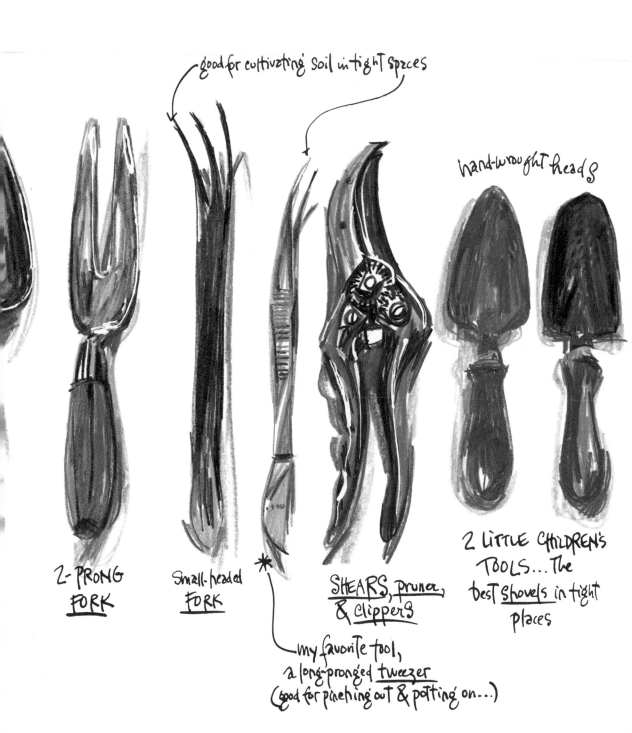

good for cultivating soil in tight spaces

hand-wrought heads

2-PRONG
FORK

Small-headed
FORK

＊

SHEARS, pruner,
& clippers

2 LITTLE CHILDREN'S
TOOLS... The
best shovels in tight
places

my favorite tool,
a long-pronged tweezer
(good for pinching out & potting on...)

Pots

USED TO BE IF I COULDN'T SCRUB THE HISTORY OUT OF SOME antique in the sanitizing cycle of my dishwasher, I wasn't interested. But ever since my horticultural psyche got in the way, I have to admit that in the garden, the older it is the better it looks. ✄ Take trees. That's what landscapers are busy doing right now. Fall is moving season once the deciduous ones have dropped their leaves and there's a client hot for an allée of hundred-year-old oaks, or maybe a little four-story-high sugar maple number to give the property some airs. Not so long ago American Indians planted saplings for their heirs. ✄ Sure you can have a garden by sundown. But rusty gate finials, chipped corners where

moss gains a foothold, trees bent by wind, or walls of ivy softening the edges of architecture—what Hollywood calls "character lines"—those only come with time. ✒ Remember how the English in the seventeenth century went off to the Continent, and overnight the landscape of the gentry sported ancestral pedigrees? Temples, obelisks, castles, statues, Greek peristyles, even arches with inscriptions in funny languages. Nothing beats the poetic look of decay like major ruins. ✒ From posh antique stores to curbside freebies, I collect ruins to ground my garden wherever they're waiting for me. ✒ I've got limestone urns and soapstone ones, and in a pair of early-nine-teenth-century English fluted urns I've got 'King George' creeping over the edge of egg-and-dart rims. That's a named variety of semper-vivum, but even better, it's the exact color of rust. This summer, two very hardy—so they say, I'll let you know in May—semi-globed box-woods, *Buxus microphylla* 'Morris Midget', were planted in aggregate urns. Pewter and bronze prehistoric-looking lichen now polka-dot the surface, and I'm doing whatever it takes to keep them going into the next century. ✒ But most of my plants that come in for the winter grow in clay. That's terra cotta, as in terra firma or, in my case, ter-race. I've got pots so big they'd humble Hercules, as well as wee-bitty ones—they used to call them "thumb pots"—alluding to Mr. McGregor's garden. The translucent French varieties—pale pink and smooth as flesh—were picked up on the last day of a trip to the South of France, and look like they were meant for the soft gray green hue of my lavender and santolina topiaries. A whole batch of sturdy, darker, rounded-rimmed pots, some numbered according to size or what the wet clay weighed when it was thrown, came from Windsor

"No sharply defined lines mark the sudden transition from the formality of architecture to the irregularity of nature."
(Frederick Law Olmsted, 19th c. American landscape designer)

"A ruin is a sacred thing. We consider it as a work of nature, rather than art."
(William Gilpin, author of books on natural scenery that influenced English picturesque gardening in the 18th c.)

"The New York skyline which, without exaggeration, is the most wonderful building district in the world, is more than half architectural terra cotta."
("The New York Times," 1911)

"There is nothing reasonable or lovable or British about a clay pot." (Roy Elliott, "Gardener's Chronicle," 1964)

Castle after they started using plastic pots for propagating and decided to clean house. My Long Toms, as in long-john underwear, hold plants with dangling taproots, but also clutch bouquets of colored pencils upstairs and down, all around my apartment because who knows where I'll be drawing next. ⅍ Frost-free alpine pans and square seed-trays used to sit on growing tables of Edwardian greenhouses; now I've got them lounging on a ledge above the city, hugging shallow-rooted sempervivum and their masses of spreading rosettes. They're outside, in full sun and hailstorms, year round because their name means they'll "live forever." And what gardener doesn't push the envelope? ⅍ The three best antique troughs I ever unearthed—the kind you picture pigs and sheep hanging around—came from Bloomingdale's. You know, the store feeding the urban clotheshorse. Any time I found myself tempted by gift-with-purchase from cosmetics on the first floor, I'd ride up and check out the crusty troughs I was keeping my eye on, right next to the escalators on the fourth floor. Lucky Pierre, they were going nowhere fast. Or in retailing lingo, "occupying valuable real estate." That's the kind of purchase a buyer makes that has the comptroller sweating. So when I offered to get all three sitting-around-ol'-pieces-of-stone-just-collecting-dust (and with luck some moss and lichen too) out of her department by tomorrow, it was a wrap. ⅍ Then how about the time the very generous Hollywood hoohaw decided a screening room would make better use of outdoor space and offered me his baker's dozen of gorgeous stone planters, the ones with Leo heads looking you in the eye. To this day I thank St. Dorothea, patroness of gardeners, he wasn't CEO of MGM. 🌿 It's all relative. I prefer the green glow from the screen of my Smith Corona. I don't have a TV and haven't found a good enough reason to get one since I drew along with Jon Gnagy on Saturday mornings at grandma's house because grandma was the only one in the family with a television. Nowadays if I want to catch some live action I watch my garden grow. 🌿

A bunch of bees drinking the catmint. No wonder it's called "Blue Wonder."

Thanksgiving Day

THE SKY'S GRAYER THAN I LIKE BUT IT'S NOT WINDY AND THEY say it won't rain, so I'm getting my stuff together. It's Thanksgiving morning and I'm looking at a list where the first page has things-to-do I should have done in September. ✹ The fourth Thursday in November is dedicated to a bird. And when it comes out of the oven, if it isn't juicy enough, if the skin's not crisp, or there's too little white meat to go around, suddenly you've got a table full of turkey mavens. Except for a meal, the rest of the holiday was always without distinction or direction, but this year I've got big plans. ✹ I'll have some breakfast with Alfonso. It was going to be toasted English muffins and we'd finish off the last jar of my homemade quince preserve, but when I discovered I'm out of sugar maybe I won't do the hot chocolate from scratch the way I wanted. I thought I'd give it a try ever since Anne-Marie sent the box of cocoa from Austria because she said the drawing on the front—with the way the steam is rising—reminded her of something I once drew. Then the rest of the day and all day Friday, Saturday, and Sunday, I'll garden, draw, and write. Maybe not your idea of celebrating, but I'm up to here with thanks. Call me a glutton, this is one feast there's no way of sharing. ✹ Over on the other side of the park I see the helium balloons above the tree line. When I was a little girl and we lived off Central Park West, Thanksgiving was when they used to leave the cars parked where they were even though there were going to be floats, marching bands, and everything. The thing I remember most, and I must have been really

"There is something to be said for being chronically short of time and breath." (Roger Swain, "Groundwork," 1994)

"When I'm in the garden I'm actually also writing. I do the equivalent of revising in the garden, continuously. I never stop digging up beds, rearranging everything." (Jamaica Kincaid, Writer, 1996)

"It may be true, as I believe it is, that the natural form of

A tree is the most beautiful possible for that particular tree, but it may happen that we do not want the most beautiful form, but one of our own designing and expressive of our ingenuity." (Shirley Hibberd, Victorian gardening author)

little because my father was still alive, is holding his hand and walking to the corner and him standing me on a car to watch the parade with a bunch of other kids. The next thing the hood caved in, and every Thanksgiving it's what I remember most. ✍ This year the parade is the background and Alfonso and I are the foreground, wrapping the boxwood pyramids with burlap. We close the package at the top with twine and then tie little twist 'ems along the stakes, and when I find my embroidery needle with the enormous eye I was sure I lost, we sew a running stitch with five-ply jute through the hanging-down material, then make a couple of knots. The wind is starting to show muscle and I see that the Pink Panther float across the park is having its own problems. But two of the four boxwoods are done, so I grace their corners with a finial from my heavy-rock collection, courtesy of Central Park. ✍ Up to now my attitude about winter was like everything else that gets me nervous: Ignore it for as long as you can. I tell myself, If junipers enjoy a good hit of fresh air and the taxus hedge survives in spite of windburn, cool it. But the boxwoods, both *Buxus sempervirens* and *Buxus microphylla,* especially when they're growing in containers, are finicky beauties, and I'm asking them to tough it out. The burlap is not insulation from the cold. The brown wrapping material is breathable protection from the devastating combination of winter windburn and sun-scalding that can dry up the small evergreen leaves, making them so brittle that come next spring they'll look like topiaries left over from Christmas decorations. I want to give my boxwoods their best shot at survival even though I agree with Christopher Lloyd that "gardeners should grow what grows well for them." ✍ By the time we stopped for breakfast, I had two tepees

"The culture of plants in our winter garden is simplicity itself, as long as we stick to the one simple rule born of our earlier failures: If it doesn't thrive, chuck it."
(Wayne Winterrowd and Joe Eck, "A Year at North Hill," 1995)

out there. They looked right, which made me think I was doing okay. But just because something looks good doesn't mean it's right. All afternoon I was making myself crazy. Should the burlap go up to the top or not? Should the tepees be open or closed? I had the perfect excuse to call someone I used to garden with who gardens for a living and could give me the answer in a hot second. But probably box-woods weren't all I wanted us to talk about. 🌿 I felt confused, like what the hell am I doing? I should just cut my losses, stick with the safe stuff, grow plants that next spring will be saying, "It's good to be back." 🌿 That's when I looked up Joey's home phone number. Not the beeper one I call when he's on a job. I figured that being it was a national day of rest, Joey would be home regrouting his fire-place or repaving the driveway—or wrapping his fig tree. Joey's a plasterer who can make walls smooth as marble—without sanding, that's the catch. Joey's also one of my kind of people, spends more time doing the prep than the actual work. He'll cover wood floors with heavy rolls of construc-tion paper and pay special attention to taping it down between the seams, then he'll put drop cloths and plastic tarps over all my books and over the bed and sofa before he hangs sheets of plastic so he's working in a bubble. Whenever Joey was rebuilding another part of my apartment because I had a new leak as soon as they dammed up the old one, we'd get to talking, and you know how it is with gardeners. One thing leads to another and the next thing you're on com-mon ground. He'd tell me about his fig tree, and fig trees aren't hardy in Queens where he lives, the way they are where he comes from in Sicily. ❧ I called him later that afternoon, and Joey said he was planning to wrap the fig tomorrow because he was still short some materials. "First," he says, "I'll take the pipe." ❧ "Pipe?" ❧ "Yeah. Pipe, poles, you know." ❧ "Oh. You mean posts. Like wooden posts." ❧ "No. Like pipe. Pipes. Metal ones." ❧ "Oh. Rebar." ❧ "Yeah. You take some pipes—five—five are okay. You hit them in the ground." ❧ "What?" ❧ "Yeah. Stand them up. Around the tree. But not too close. Then take a piece of canvas." ❧ "Canvas?" ❧ "Yeah, like a drop cloth, the one like I use on your sofa. You wrap it around the poles around the tree. Then you close it." ❧ "With what?" ❧ "With duck tape." ❧ "Duck tape?" ❧ "Yeah, you know, the silver tape." ❧ "Oh! You mean duct tape, Joey." ❧ "Yeah, duck tape. Then you go around with the wrap insulation." ❧ "The what?" ❧ "You know, it's on a roll, it comes with the aluminum foil on one side. Keeps the tree nice and warm inside. Then you close it." ❧ "With duck tape." ❧ "*Right.* Next comes the roofing paper." ❧ "Roofing paper?" ❧ "Yeah. Stuff some plastic bags in the top, then put the roofing paper over it. Then cover the whole thing with a big garbage bag." ❧ "Huh?" ❧ "Yeah. Because in the spring you take everything off and you can throw it in the garbage bag. Nice and neat. The way I leave your place. Just remember you gotta do it before the tree starts vegetating." ❧ The fig jam his family makes— Joey calls it honey—that he gives everyone for Christmas came from last year's crop from his eight-year-old fig tree. ❧ Nowadays, you want a bit of Eden, you gotta do the prep. ❧

And "the fig tree puts forth its figs." (The Song of Solomon, 2:8-13)

Quince

I SMELL QUINCE, THE GOLDEN APPLE THEY SAY STARTED ALL the problems. ⚘ We're into the shortest days of fall and I'm standing in the Bonnefont Herb Garden at the Cloisters where the four best fruit trees growing in Manhattan are looking very Garden of Eden-ish. ⚘ There are covered walkways surrounding open courtyards, and for a reality check the drone of traffic from the West Side Highway hums in the background. The Cloisters is a branch of the Metropolitan Museum of Art, and was originally designed and planted in 1938, the same year the museum opened. Thirteenth-century portals, marble columns, carved capitals with spiny acanthus leaves or jumping monkeys—all came from a bunch of real cloisters in the South of France. So did the walls and vaulted ceilings of massive limestone block, and also the stairs, which are worn away in the middle even though they're solid slabs of stone. ⚘ Every bit of this architecture was disassembled, shipped over, then put together again—better than Humpty Dumpty—perched above Manhattan Island on a hill in Fort Tryon Park. The whole damn place is so evocative, it's hard to believe that the Number Four bus takes me to the door. ⚘ But I'm worried I might be too late to draw the quinces still on the trees as soon as I hear the medieval music and see that they're putting up the garlands of boxwood with hazelnuts and apples. The eight-foot wreath of wheat—now that's something they should sell for Christmas—is criss-crossed with crimson cloth and hangs flat like a giant angel's halo. They've also covered the Venetian wellhead in the center of the herb

Cydonia oblonga is not everyone's favorite in the fruit-of-the-month club, so any commercial grower with his eye on staying in business better grow good-looking fruit. I'd bought three quinces—or about two pounds if you're following the recipe—from an untouched carton of perfectly round, greenish yellow beauties, all with shine and very little fuzz but, thank Pomona, goddess of fruit trees, they still had aroma. ⁒ After a Cloisters morning and feeling medieval all over and visiting my favorite quince trees with ancient-looking trunks that could have played the opening scene in Genesis, I'm in the mood to make a Mexican dessert called Paradise Jelly. But with all that testing for sugar-ball stage and everything, I go back to my simple Owl and Pussycat Preserve. Again and again. ⁒ On the way home I notice that they're selling Christmas trees with pre-strung lights. You could have fooled me, since I always thought the best part about Christmas trees was the ritual. Finding the right one, getting it through the doorway without losing all the needles, then setting it up. Serve the tree some water, pour a drink for yourself, then you and the branches can both relax. ⁒ When you're ready, you take out the box with the ornaments from that place you visit once a year—the top shelf in the closet, or maybe under the bed. With people who feel the way you do about these kinds of things, you spend the rest of the night doing show-and-tell on each and every tchotchke before hanging it up. ⁒ I make my quince preserve every year—at the end of autumn—because no matter how the light is changing, there's permanence in the rituals. Nothing is different, yet all the buds are going to be new. ⁒

that Quinces Promoted cheerfulness.

"I enjoy cooking very much. It goes with a garden rather well."
(Christopher Lloyd, interview 1986)

Epilogue

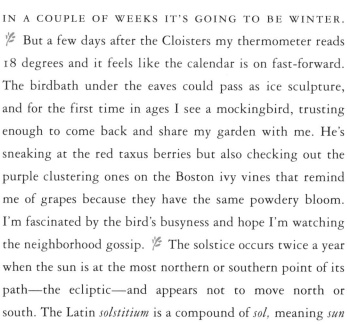

IN A COUPLE OF WEEKS IT'S GOING TO BE WINTER.
🌿 But a few days after the Cloisters my thermometer reads
18 degrees and it feels like the calendar is on fast-forward.
The birdbath under the eaves could pass as ice sculpture,
and for the first time in ages I see a mockingbird, trusting
enough to come back and share my garden with me. He's
sneaking at the red taxus berries but also checking out the
purple clustering ones on the Boston ivy vines that remind
me of grapes because they have the same powdery bloom.
I'm fascinated by the bird's busyness and hope I'm watching
the neighborhood gossip. 🌿 The solstice occurs twice a year
when the sun is at the most northern or southern point of its
path—the ecliptic—and appears not to move north or
south. The Latin *solstitium* is a compound of *sol,* meaning *sun*
(like *parasol, solar,* and *solarium*), and *sistere,* meaning *standing* or *stop-*
page (like *armistice*). The winter solstice is the shortest day of the
year, when light seems to have stopped. But after December 21, the
elastic moments of morning and night will start changing places. 🌿

The rhythms of nature bring us back to center. With age-old reverence for the mysteries of vegetation, we hear the Earth breathing. Dormant buds are becoming restless even as snow swaddles the ground. And so am I. 🌿 The garden is a fugitive art, it comes and goes. Neglect one for just a few years and things will revert, not that anything's wrong with wilderness. But like I said in the very beginning, nature doesn't make gardens. We do. Plantings occur by chance out there, and though they can be exquisite, sometimes we want it our way. 🌿 How else can you explain that when Adam and Eve were expelled from Paradise, not only did they take wheat, chief of foods, and the date, chief of fruits, but they also carried a branch from an evergreen bush of true myrtle for everlasting beauty? *Myrtus communis* has the sweetest smelling leaves, the most aromatic puffs of small white flowers. Even the wood is fragrant. And if you grow it right, you'll have a little tree. 🌿 Makes me think maybe we need a garden, much as it needs us. 🌿

"There is a beautiful house with many gardens in your future." (Lucky numbers 2, 54, 34, 48, 27, 10) (Fortune cookie, 1995)

Acknowledgments

Like a garden, many elements create a book. To everyone who helped me cultivate these pages, this bouquet is for you. ✿ Thank you to Jen Bilik, a unique editor, and Charles Miers, a rare publisher, both of whom are as intensely interested in the final work as I am. And Bonnie Eldon, Elizabeth White, and Belinda Hellinger, my caring and concerned co-workers at Universe Publishing; John Brancati at Rizzoli Bookstores; and St. Martin's Press—thank you one and all for intelligent advice, but especially your enthusiasm and support. ✿ For their sensitivity in handling my material, thank you to Barbara Sturman, Karla Eoff, Joanna Lehan, and Leah Fitschen. And thank you to the whole graveyard shift at Kinko's, especially Shabazz Head. ✿ For answering my questions and responding with so much more than I asked for, thank you to Bradford Lyon and Joanne Fuccello at Elisabeth Woodburn Books, Penny Reichard at Capability's Books, and Katherine Powis, librarian at the New York Horticultural Society. ✿ Thank you to Mary Flower for handling the legal matters, and Lilibeth Felisarta for handling the household. Also to Brother Anthony for encouraging me to use the quote cited at his invocation for my own dedication page; and to everyone else I quoted, living or from other centuries; and to Chris Giftos, manager of special events at the Metropolitan Museum of Art, for his breathtaking flower arrangements and for permitting me to document them at eight in the morning. Ever since I was a staff artist for a daily newspaper, it's been my favorite way to work: from life, a bit uncomfortable, and in a rush. ✿ In addition, I thank my garden of friends: Mary Albi, Larry Ashmead, Suzanne Bonté, Diane Cohen and Ed Koones, Anne-Marie Colban, Mary Ehni, Kevin Esteban, Marty Gluck, Allen Haskell, Nancy Klein, Otis, Sarah Peter, Janee Ries, Suzanne Slesin, Sally Schermerhorn, and Ed Wilkin. And Joan Klein. Besides her friendship, I'm grateful to Tovah Martin for her botanical editing. Also to Alfonso Flores, who looks forward to working in my garden as much as I do. And thank you Jerry Wilson for leading me into the garden. ✿ For that loving creature Timothy, I will always grow a special little bouquet of catmint. ✿

"What is the use of a book," thought Alice, "without pictures

Colophon

The text for this book is set in Garamond No. 3. Claude Garamond was an independent punchcutter who was commissioned by the French royal court to create fonts in the sixteenth century, the golden age of French typography. In 1917, Garamond No. 3 was issued by the American Type Founders, based on the Garamond-inspired designs of Morris F. Benton, T. M. Cleland, and Jean Jannon. The issue led to an international, twentieth-century Garamond revival; the Frenchman's fonts remain among the most popular of this century. The dingbats are some of my own botanical doodles, and the hand-lettering is "Abbie Zabar Display," done with my favorite old-fashioned nib, a Hunt 101. The line drawings also use that pen, or a .35 Rapidograph. All of my color drawings, including the cover lettering, were done with Berol Prismacolor pencils and Pentel Fine Point Correction Pen on any piece of paper that was handy at the time. The layouts were composed on the Macintosh computer in Quark XPress; the images were scanned in Adobe Photoshop. The cover paper is a special Italian stock called Tintoretto.

r conversations?" (Lewis Carroll's "Alice's Adventures in Wonderland," 1865)

From the Garden
Library
of

....